Aleister Crowley:
Man, Myth & Magick

Steven Ashe
Warburg-Maple 2015

Aleister Crowley: Man, Myth & Magick

ISBN: 978-1515228134

For Merl
(Steve Harrington)

1 Towards the Golden Dawn

Even over a half a century after his death, the legend of Aleister Crowley haunts the histories of the world of occultism. His biographers can't agree whether he was a genuine spiritual visionary, seeking expression through poetic mediumship and ritual magic, or simply an eccentric genius, employing his esoteric interests as a cover for diplomatic espionage on his many world travels. The general public don't know if to be more impressed that Led Zeppelin guitarist Jimmy Page is one of the world's most enthusiastic collectors of Crowley's works and purchased his Loch Ness mansion or by the fact that his life long notoriety as 'The Wickedest Man in the World' led to the inclusion of his portrait amongst those assembled on the cover of The Beatles Sgt Pepper Album. Crowley's admirers include several rock and pop music personalities who have referenced him in their work from Graham Bond to David Bowie. The Mountaineer Chris Bonnington is also a fan - for Crowley set several mountaineering altitude and endurance records on his Himalayan adventures - and

Aleister Crowley: Man, Myth & Magick

Aldous Huxley, author of The Doors of Perception, whom he turned-on to Mescalin in the 1930s, thought highly of him as a man of ideas.

Ask almost anyone their view on Aleister Crowley and opinions will polarize: he was a genius; a psychopath; a drug riddled sex maniac; a champion of sexual freedom against the restrictions of Victorian prudery and hypocrisy; he was a secret agent; a lost-soul poet; a playboy with little better to do than dabble in magic; a lifestyle imitator of Oscar Wilde and Richard Burton; a drug addict; a narcissistic sadist; a visionary artist; a parasitic leech on the charity of his friends and followers. Even in contemporary times one of his more intellectual American 'heirs' claims him as an authentic Satanist whilst others choose to whitewash their interpretation of Aleister Crowley's spiritual literary output in the clearest of radiant light. In both instances, for many adherents Aleister Crowley has seemingly apotheosized into a controversial religious figurehead if not into the prophet of a modern cult.

Many practitioners of the rites of modern Wicca are completely in denial that 'The Craft's' Book of Shadows, revealed to the world by Gerald Gardner, has proven to be in Crowley's unmistakable style Modern students of Hermeticism and the study of the ritual magic of medieval grimoires are also often at pains to distance themselves from the reputation of the man. His open minded approach to uniting the spiritual mysteries of the West with elder Eastern and Tantric sexual lore tends to jar with their preference for a European based Gnostic heritage. Yet without the impact of Aleister Crowley's prolific publishing initiatives, the rites and magical teachings of the influential Victorian era Order of the Golden Dawn would never have reached the public at large. He was the first to publish the key rituals and teachings of this influential magical order and even the later publication of the full curriculum of the Golden Dawn was executed by Israel Regardie, one of his students.

Quite separate to his career as an innovator of modern occult practices, Aleister Crowley worked hard to develop his vocation as a poet and had work published in The Oxford Book of

Mystical Verse and The Occult Review. His two novels, Moonchild and Diary of a Drug Fiend brought him no great commercial success and as far as his magical and mystical writings were concerned he was effectively self-published, spending large amounts on lavish hardback first editions of his early works - with the binding and spine-leather of each edition emblazoned in specific colours thought to be magically significant to the nature of the volume in hand.

A gifted individual, from a well to do upper middle class family tainted with a belief in the literal truth of every word of the King James Bible, the young Aleister found his escape from the mental straightjacket of family religious observances and the sadistic bigotry of the English private schools through the outlets of Chess and Mountaineering.

Between the years 1891 and 1897, he had climbed the most challenging peaks in Scotland and the Swiss Alps including the first unguided ascent of the Mönch and the Eiger. The adolescent Crowley wrote a list of his mountaineering conquests and applied to the

Scottish Mountaineering Club for membership. He was accepted by a ballot of the members at a special meeting convened on December 7th 1894. Earlier in that year, Crowley had attended Eastbourne College on the south coast of England for the Spring and Summer terms, where he assumed leadership of the town's Chess Club and wrote a Wednesday evening chess column for the Eastbourne Gazette. He occupied his remaining leisure hours climbing the chalk cliff at Beachy Head, previously considered unclimable.

The following year, Crowley began his studies at Cambridge University having secured the recommendation of British Prime Minister Lord Salisbury, a family friend, with a view to joining the Diplomatic Service following graduation. The young man's application for admission to Trinity College was also supported by Charles Thomson Ritchie, former Secretary to the Admiralty. This connection between the Crowley family and the diplomatic service would be continued by Crowley, who later counted Ian Fleming, who served in Naval Intelligence during World War Two, as a friend. Another close acquaintance, Everard Feilding, the Secretary of the celebrated Society for Psychical Research, was a highly decorated ex-military aide in the Diplomatic Service who served as Crowley's handler during his career as an agent of British Intelligence from 1914 onwards.

During the course of World War One, informed commentators such as Dr Richard Spence and Tobias Churton maintain that Crowley's activities in New York writing pro-German propaganda and burning his British passport in a publicly advertised display beneath the Statue of Liberty provided cover for covert operations undermining pro-Irish Republican organizations on the east coast of the United States. Strangely enough, it is a matter of public record that the US State Department, who were aware of Crowley's influence upon the New York-Boston pro-German propaganda secretariat, were under orders from the British Consul to leave him alone as he was listed as an employee of the British government.

During World War Two, some thirty years later, one of Crowley's libertarian poems was adopted by General DeGaulle, set to music and broadcast on BBC radio. Recent historians such as Churton have also confirmed as true the prior 'myth' that it was Crowley who influenced Churchill to make popular the V for Victory hand sign as a sign of resistance during the wartime years. His involvement in the evaluation of the testimony of Rudolph Hesse, Hitler's Deputy who parachuted into Scotland to negotiate a separate peace with England, is also reportedly whispered of in intelligence circles.

Considering the curious combination of having elite political family connections, a penchant for global travel and exploration, a Cambridge University education and having inherited enough money to live the life of an Edwardian Gentleman of leisure, recent academic opinion tends to favour the notion that Aleister Crowley was a life-long Agent of the British Crown. Whilst mountaineering and chess remained lifelong passions, and though the magical and mystical quest was ever present in his poetic and literary output, many of Crowley's global explorations and spiritual pilgrimages to the far flung borders of the British Empire are remarkably convergent with areas of specific interest to the Foreign Policy of the British

Government at the time.

Crowley's association with the world of magic and occultism is a whole area of study in itself. Again, it is one of those many areas of interest in his life which is open to misinterpretation and misrepresentation by those who remain in ignorance of the cultural and personal motivations which he strived to live up to and measure himself by.

Born Edward Alexander Crowley in Leamington, 1875, the son of an upper middle class civil engineer and a professional governess, the young Aleister was raised in privileged circumstances. His father's cousin was the founder of Crowley's Old Ale Brewery, who owned half of the town of Alton, Hampshire and the family money was choicely invested in the concern. This was a brewery of industrial scale and, by the time shareholdings had forced control from the family into the hands of private shareholders around 1870, Edward Crowley senior was able to dispose of his interests and secure the small fortune of which his son would later inherit his share.

Steven Ashe

Aleister was to lose his father soon after his eleventh birthday, later citing the misdiagnosis of a cancer condition as the leading cause of this tragic event. When a dominant uncle, a strict religious disciplinarian, stepped in to manage the household's affairs following their bereavement Crowley was sent packing to a series of boarding schools which characterized what he later described as a 'boyhood in Hell'. At a school in Cambridge specifically for children of Plymouth Brethren he was 'sent to Coventry' for an entire term, an experience involving no student or staff member being allowed to talk directly to him or even acknowledge his existence; including maintaining their silence upon the very accusation which the young Crowley was expected to intuit and admit voluntarily. A malicious student had reported to the hysterical headmaster that he had witnessed Crowley drunk, although the unfortunate innocent only learned of the charge after leaving the 'care' of the establishment. Fed on bread and water as punishment for a term and a half, the young student became ill with a seriously debilitating kidney disease and was removed by his Uncle, Tom Bishop whose affectation for blinkered religious hypocrisy fortunately did not extend to turning a blind eye to life threatening sadism.

When Crowley matriculated at Trinity College Cambridge, and soon after came into his inheritance, he was at last able to free himself from the psychological straightjacket of family life in the Plymouth Brethren which had contrived to restrict his natural emotional development at every opportunity. In his early years his mother had hysterically referred to him as the Beast of Revelation, sent to try her, for simply asking her about ladies legs. "Ladies do not have legs," she primly replied. The imp Crowley had other ideas and disappeared beneath the dinner table when female guests were in attendance to arise and embarassingly announce to the entire table that his mother's guests were not ladies.

At Cambridge, Crowley skipped lectures and read the Classics from his own personal library, setting his own reading program. Passing his term exams was a breeze and the young scholar maintained luxurious apartments, lived the good life which, even today, is only truly available to the young and financially privileged. Signing the Cambridge Roll as Edward Aleister Crowley, he registered as a student of Trinity College on the same day as Charles Stewart Rolls, the founder of Rolls-Royce. He bought a car. Doing his utmost to escape the contempt of upper class elitism, hostile to his middle-class family background, Crowley began to expend his considerable fortune upon entertaining and generally making a splash. He won one wager in which he gambled with his friends that he could afford to take all of them to lunch and dinner in town, every day for a whole week. When the bill was presented at the end of each meal, the young wag would pull out a fifty pound note, a huge sum of money for the era, only to be informed that the establishment did not have sufficient cash to make change. Crowley simply signed the bill, returning to pay for each meal at the end of the week from the proceeds of his winnings.

The close of 1896 found the neophyte Diplomat in Stockholm where he was introduced personally to the British Consular staff. Having come into his inheritance on 12th October, Crowley no longer needed family permission for his foreign adventures. On New Year's Eve he found himself seduced by a Scotsman, James L. Dickson into a passive liaison of gay sex. Writing about this in his later autobiography, 'The Confessions of Aleister Crowley', he dresses this adventure in symbolic language:

"I was awakened to the knowledge that I possessed a magical means of becoming conscious of and satisfying a part of my nature which had up to that moment concealed itself from me. It was an experience of horror and pain, combined with a certain ghostly terror, yet at the same time it was the key to the purest and holiest spiritual ecstasy that exists. At the time, I was not aware of the supreme importance of the matter. It seemed to me little more than a development of certain magical processes with which I was already familiar; it was an isolated experience, not repeated until exactly twelve months later, to the minute."

In 1897 he travelled to St Petersburg, Russia, giving the excuse of further preparation for his career in the Diplomatic Service in 'The Confessions of Aleister Crowley. Here, he hoped to improve his command of spoken Russian. Apart from observing a Berlin Chess championship whilst en route back to his homeland, Crowley found the adventure lackluster. He grew swiftly disenchanted with the plans of mortal men and made a decision to abandon any ambitions for an official career in Diplomacy and from this point onwards intensified his ambitions towards influencing world affairs through cultural and spiritualistic stratagems.

The call to the path of poetry had gripped Crowley since his juvenile years. The call of literature and revolutionary poetry as the Rock Music industry of its day was appealing to his youthful mind. Byron had established the poet as anti-hero nearly a hundred years before and in France, two decades previously, Rimbaud had granted the poet the status of crazy-wisdom mystic as he had sought to gain visionary potency through the breaking of cultural taboo and poetic transcendence through the derangement of the senses. Oscar Wilde was fading in a living literary martyrdom in Paris, but a thriving demi-monde atmosphere was seeping across the English Channel from the French city of light. Paris was in the mid stages of la Belle Époque and the Art clique with whom Crowley found himself rubbing shoulders in the Halls of Cambridge included Gerald Kelly, later President of the Royal Society of Arts, who was to introduce the young poet personally to the Artist Rodin and the Bohemian garrets of the Left Bank of the Seine. Kelly would later become Crowley's reluctant Brother in Law.

In 1898, before leaving Cambridge, Crowley paid a local printer to publish his first poetic work 'Aceldema: A Place to Bury Strangers' under the anonymous legend 'By a Gentleman of the University of Cambridge'. In an earlier age, Shelley had published his own premiere masterpiece under the by-line of '...a Gentleman of the University of Oxford'.

Along with evolving fashions in Art and literature, one consequence of the explosion of French new-romanticism in British popular culture was a surge of interest in magic and mysticism. The intellectuals of France had for some two decades stolen a lead on their British counterparts in this area. The celebrated French mystic Eliphas Levi had died some six months prior to Crowley's birth and the artists of Paris had already delivered a number of sophisticated post-modern Tarot Decks as the end of the century approached.

Coming across an early edition of Arthur Edward Waite's 'Book of Black Magic and Pacts' early in 1898 Crowley seized upon the world of magic as a source of fresh poetic inspiration and wrote to the author for guidance. Waite had hinted at the existence of a sovereign sanctuary of the Elect and the young poet was inquisitive as to where he might find such an august and arcane body. Waite wrote back, recommending the young man to study von Eckarthausen's translation of the Eastern classic 'The Cloud upon the Sanctuary', a work very much in vogue with the European intelligentsia particularly in Russia, where the Tsar himself was said to be enthusiastic about the work. The underlying premise of the text describes an invisible school of esoteric Masters whose concealed hand guides the historical development of world affairs. This was music to Crowley's ears as it appealed to his notions of an aristocracy of the spirit and as being quite in line with the Platonic ideals of his classical education. He threw himself into occult studies, beginning with a thorough investiation into the ancient art of Alchemy; quite in harmony with his prior reading in Chemistry which constituted the major area of his university studies.

In April, he met Oscar Eckenstein on an Easter visit to Wastdale Head and began a complex relationship with this older man whose talent for rock climbing equaled his own but whose wealth of experience dazzled him. Crowley later considered Eckenstein the greatest climber in Europe. He recounts that Eckenstein could with ease get a grip on a ledge, which could only be truly considered a ledge by a man far gone under the influence of Hashish, and be sitting on it smoking his pipe five minutes later. Eckenstein was involved in several later mountaineering expeditions with Crowley in the Alps and the Himalayas and is credited with the invention of the modern climbing crampon.

Meeting Eckenstein was key to Crowley's later development as a mystic and a magician. For the better part of the next decade, he would respect Eckenstein's guidance. His diaries and journals make clear homosexual encounters were a semi regular feature of their relationship.

At the time of their meeting the young poet had found himself head over heels in love with Herbert Jerome Pollitt, an older fellow Cambridge student who had taken to the stage as a female impersonator. At a cusp in his relationship with Pollitt, Crowley threw him over for the company of Eckenstein and climbing expeditions in the Alps. He lived to later express regret for this decision and to rail against the hostility society reserved for homosexuality which ultimately guided his choice and perhaps robbed him of an honest expression of his inner leanings.

In July, whilst climbing in Zermatt, Switzerland, Crowley discovered S.L. Mathers' 'Kabbalah Denudata' or 'Kabbalah Unveiled' and as the August weather proved fruitful for climbing, Crowley extended his ambitions and became a Minor cause-celebre amongst the Alpine community for his exploits on the ice-face. Whilst discoursing upon the finer points of Alchemy over a round of drinks one evening, the young adventurer fell into conversation with Julian Baker, a medical Doctor whose knowledge of Alchemy exceeded his own. Was this the master Crowley was seeking? Baker claimed not to be, but knew of one who might be called master - namely one George Cecil Jones of Basingstoke, an analytical chemist and one of Baker's peers in the Hermetic Order of the Golden Dawn, a magical society currently being administered by Mathers, author of The Kabbalah Unveiled.

Crowley took the bait and, upon returning to England, made the acquaintance of Jones with whom he continued to work in a fluid partnership for many years to come, despite the cataclysmic upheavals and scandals which the Golden Dawn order would experience in the following decade.

Under the sponsorship of Jones and under the watchful eye of Florence Farr, Crowley underwent the initiation rite of Neophyte before the gathered dignitaries of the Golden Dawn on November 18th, 1898 at Mark Masons Hall, London. Less than two weeks later, involving another magical ceremony, Crowley was initiated into the Zelator grade and began his studies in Astral Travel and Magic in seriousness under the tutelage of George Cecil Jones.

Steven Ashe

After Crowley's third ceremony of initiation into the spiritual grade of Theoricus, early in 1899, he was approached by one of the more earnest magicians of the Golden Dawn, Alan Bennett who inquired as to whether or not the young aspirant had been dabbling with the Goetia, the hollow shells of 'demonic' form. Upon issuing a denial, the aspiring novice was told by Bennett, in that case, the Goetia were surely dabbling with him. Intrigued, Crowley quickly took to Bennett who was in a state of severe debilitation of health through chronic asthma and also dire financial impoverishment.

Bennett was no slouch intellectually and, by profession, an electrical engineer. He was considered to be one of Golden Dawn chief Mathers' leading pupils, only the London fog and damp exacerbated his asthma and consequently put the brakes on his social and economic mobility. To the young Crowley's credit, in a selfless act of generosity, he proposed that Bennett share his luxurious apartments and benefit from his good fortune whilst he would take payment for lodgings and hospitality in the form of lessons in Golden

Dawn curriculum magic from the more experienced mage. A bargain was struck, and thus began one of the more curious episodes of experimentation in magic in the history of late Victorian England.

In the mainstream of the membership the Golden Dawn novice would be introduced to the concepts underlying the study of western hermetic magic via rites of ceremonial theatre.

This curriculum included familiarity with the nature of the alchemic elements, the importance of the Hebrew letters to the biblical narrative of Creation and their relationship to the paths of the Qabalistic Tree of Life and the study of Geomancy and Tarot. In addition, a range of magical lore borrowed wholesale from the medieval writings of Cornelius Agrippa and the later collections of Francis Barrett, compiled in his edition of *The Magus* formed the backbone of necessary study in the Hermetic Golden Dawn. The work of historic continental magicians was also mined for refinements. The Latin translation of books of The Zohar by Knorr von Rosenroth, formed the basis of Mathers' own treatment of the Kabbalah. The learned Golden Dawn chief spent hours as a gentleman scholar, poring over ancient texts in the British Library and Biblioteque L'Arsenal in Paris where he unearthed such treasures as The Sacred Magic of Abramelin the Mage and several forgotten manuscripts of The Key of Solomon.

Alan Bennett's kudos within the Order lay in his close friendship with Mathers, who respected his student's opinions and his fearsome reputation as a practical magician. Like Mathers, Bennett haunted the London lodge of the Theosophical Society and would occasionally play tricks on the membership there; calling upon his electrical know-how to deliver electric shocks to individuals foolish enough to accept his invitation to touch a large crystal 'wand' he carried with him.

Bennett would eventually fall out with the Eurocentric Mathers due to his deep fascination with eastern mystical lore, taunting a very drunk Mathers into a furious rage by repeatedly chanting 'Shiva', having convinced his inebriate host that the Universe might be brought to an end by this mantra. Some twenty years hence,

Bennett would return from almost two decades of Eastern travels to form the embryonic British Buddhist movement which continues to run the public festival known as Buddha-Field in the south-west of England every summer.

That Aleister Crowley had a hand in the foundation of Buddhism in the West has to honoured. For it was Crowley who encouraged his lover to pay Bennett's fare to the Orient, and who remained a faithful friend taking care to twice visit his mentor in Ceylon in later years. Without his friends intervention Bennett's asthma would have killed him and, despite their friendship not surviving the separation of the years due to Crowley being in America and then Sicily upon Bennett's return from the East, Crowley always looked upon his memories of Alan Bennett fondly.

Living as an odd couple in Crowley's apartments at 67-69 Chancery Lane afforded the two magicians the leisure to practice magic and study the knowledge lectures of the Hermetic Golden Dawn on a full time basis. Bennett seems to have had a monumental effect upon Crowley, introducing him to the psycho-active effects of mind altering drugs, magic mushrooms and the smoking of Hashish. At the same time as this psychedelic tour de force was underway in the heart of genteel late 19th century London, rites of ritual magic summoning frightful spirits to materialization were also being practiced. In his autobiography Crowley writes of having maintained both a Black Magic and a White Magic Temple at the address; the Black Magic Temple being a small wardrobe containing a skeleton in which the magical duo would sacrifice the occasional pigeon or turtle dove.

The occult author Dion Fortune, writing in Psychic Self Defence, recounts Crowley's tales of armies of dispossessed spirits marching to and fro in his apartments during this period, causing considerable distress to his refined neighbours. Fortune, an initiate of a later manifestation of the Golden Dawn order, travelled to meet Crowley shortly before his death in the late 1940s at no small cost to her reputation.

Having formed her own offshoot of the Golden Dawn, known as the Fraternity of the Inner

Light, Dion Fortune maintained a correspondence with Aleister Crowley against the moral objections of her friends and magical allies. By this time, with a reputation as 'The Wickedest Man in the World' coined by the Sunday Express, Crowley had become a hot potato; far too hot for the comfort of the 'Tea and Cucumber Sandwich' set swelling the Christian mystical ranks of her society. Nevertheless she traveled to Hastings to meet with him and from the reports of witness Kenneth Grant - later Crowley's literary editor - the two got on like a house on fire.

Alan Bennett's relationship with Crowley was remarkably chaste. Bennett's prudery and lack of knowledge concerning reproductive sex amused his friend greatly. He recounts Bennett expressing horror that the generative organ in both sexes should be also linked to the urinary tract. An insight into Bennett's juvenile level of sexual development may also be gleaned from Crowley's autobiography where he reports that Bennett was always returning at odd times of the night in some disheveled state due to having been pursued by footpads and irate red faced men. Most probably he was a peeping tom.

Crowley's period of residence in Chancery Lane was coloured by his sense of Drama. Ostensibly, according to his own account, to impress tradesman he put it about that he was really Count Vladimir Svaroff: an alias he maintained until he left London for the Scottish Highlands later in the year. Everard Feilding, Crowley's British Intelligence contact, would comment that it was only Crowley's sense of the dramatic which had ruined what would otherwise be a series of admirable fronts for intelligence work. Some recent commentators have suggested that Crowley's alias at this time was indicative of a continuation of undercover work amongst London based revolutionary Russian emigres, conducted on behalf of his former Diplomatic Service contacts. The young pretender also found the assumed title useful in persuading tradesmen to increase his credit limit.

By May of 1899, Crowley had reached the highest grade of the Outer Order of the Golden Dawn, that of Philosophus or 4=7 (having taken the Practicus exam in February). He was now fully committed to attaining the more subtle states of preparation to enable the experience of spiritual ascension when the grade of Lesser Adept is conferred to the Golden Dawn initiate.

Despite maintaining an almost fanatical interest in the study of Golden Dawn teaching material, and having Alan's more advanced Adeptus notebooks and journals openly available to him, Crowley's advancement to the circle of the Adepti could not have been more ill timed. On the one hand, the stability of the authority of Mathers was for the first time being called into question. A fellow Adept, F.L. Gardner, had lent Mathers the sum of fifty pounds two years previously. Prior to this, Mather's had relied upon a sinecure as curator of the Horniman Museum which depended upon the good opinion of fellow Golden Dawn administratrix Annie Horniman who was also a personal friend of Mather's French wife Moina since their studies at the Slade Institute of Art.

Annie Horniman had become embroiled in an argument with Mathers over the issue of the sexual dream-magic currently being preached by fellow Golden Dawn alumnus Dr Berridge. Berridge was influenced by the teachings of the

Steven Ashe

Hermetic Brotherhood of Luxor, a group founded by Max Theon who shared an early history with Madame Blavatsky before she rejected the path of practical magic. Ms Horniman professed herself to be offended by the sexual impropriety of Berridge's teaching and forced a schism in the meetings which ultimately led to a face-off with Mathers and his consequent lack of funding. More damaging were the implications for Mathers leadership. He had borrowed what amounted to a year's wages and, in preference to playing a cautious hand, decided to thrash about and blame others for his misfortune whilst carefully dodging the debt. Unfortunately other creditors were also moving in and the magical chief was facing bankruptcy.

Crowley had just purchased Boleskine House, a palatial one story manor house facing the shores of Loch Ness. The drug fueled rowdy goings-on in his Chancery Lane apartments, plus the intrigue of sexual scandal due to his having developed a preference for scourging and bondage influenced by the writings of De Sade, had attracted a measure of police attention. Some whiff of this scandal had reached the ears of fellow Golden Dawn members and suspicions surrounding the young rake were already poisoning his chances amongst his London lodge order superiors. As Bennett and Jones, both in Mathers' camp, had facilitated Crowley's introduction to their chief, the young magicians card was already marked. When he finally met Mathers in Paris, his loyalties were declared and Crowley was personally inducted into the Rosicrucian Inner Order by Mathers himself on January 16th 1900.

Perceiving Mather's state of near penury, and feeling a natural sympathy for their plight, Crowley elected to help. Whilst the couple were in dire financial straits, they were not without influence in the French capital. Moina, Mathers' wife, was the sister of the philosopher Henri Bergson. Mathers himself maintained political connections on the extreme right-wing of European ultra-royalist political extremism and was host to a continual flow of sympathizers which ensured a thriving social dynamic. Pennywise, however, they were as poor as church mice.

In an effort to alleviate the financial strain of his

magical patrons, Crowley undertook to handle the publication of Mather's Lesser Key of Solomon and took possession of various manuscripts, some of which he later published under his own imprint. Mather's was obliged and, in April, granted Crowley nominal authority to take possession of the London Vault of the Adepti and seize the order seals. This followed the London Temple's refusal of Mathers' authority to release Adeptus Minor documents to Crowley as a newly minted Inner Order member.

Again, Crowley's sense of the dramatic lent an air of unreality to the occasion for he arrived at Golden Dawn headquarters 36 Blyth Road dressed for the occasion in a kilt of Highland tartan, a black mask and sporting a tribal dagger at his hip. The landlady considered him quite mad, as indeed did Golden Dawn officers who soon arrived on the scene. Crowley had hired a strong-arm man from a West End pub but he got lost and arrived too late to assist. Order luminary W.B. Yeats ordered the properties locks to be changed overnight. He later wrote: "Mathers sent a mad man, whom we refused to initiate, to take possession of the rooms and papers of the Society ... The envoy is really Crowley, a quite unspeakable person. He is I believe seeking vengeance for us not initiating him ... Mathers like all despots must have a favourite and this is the lad."

Returning to Boleskine on the shores of Loch Ness, Crowley decided to to duck out of the London heat. The debts he had accumulated under his aristocratic Russian pseudonym and the reputation he had been careful to cultivate were turning bad on him. A girlfriend openly confronted him with not so thinly veiled accusations of sodomy with the 'brother of a university chum'. His apartments, she told him, were under surveillance from the police. On top of this, his mistress - a woman married to a British Army Officer - approached Golden Dawn members she knew personally and informed them that Crowley had scammed her into donating fifty pounds towards Alan Bennett's passage to embark on his Eastern retreat as a Buddhist Monk in Indian Ceylon. She also spilled the beans on Crowley's inventive interpretation of more catholic aspects of De Sade's sexual interests, claiming he had hung her from skewers which penetrated her flesh in an orgy of medieval iniquity. London was scandalized and Crowley made due haste north of the border where he could lose himself in a supreme magical operation he had discussed with Mathers: the magical ritual of Abramelin the Mage, requiring six months of prayer and purification and designed to place him in touch with an entity known as the Holy Guardian Angel.

Crowley had initially purchased Boleskine House specifically with this magical operation in mind. The house itself fulfilled all the conditions stipulated in the text of the medieval grimoire, being private and facing water with hills at the rear. He had sought high and low throughout the United Kingdom for such a property and only persuaded the owner to part company with the Scottish property by offering him twice the market value.

Following a few short weeks spent decorating his new house and temple space whilst introducing himself as the new Laird to the taciturn people of the small village of Foyers, Crowley took the advice of close friends and departed Great Britain for New York. He reached the American metropolis on July 6th and doubtless breathed a sigh of relief as his planned circumnavigation of the globe would remove him from the direct scrutiny of those investigating his moral character at home. Armed with copies of Bennett's Golden Dawn papers and a small library of books, which he had taken to carrying even to the top of mountains in a trunk, the young magician looked forward to a season climbing in Mexico and then a cruise to the Far East, via Hawaii, where he would meet up with Bennett and study Yoga.

Crowley's absence from the European theatre of Golden Dawn operations during the next year and a half, or so prevented more than the embarrassment of investigation for outrage of public morals. He was also spared the indignity of finding himself in Mathers' camp during the period of scandal caused by what has come to be called the Horos affair. This ill-fated turn of events brought what remained of the public Golden Dawn into shame and disrepute.

Two confidence tricksters had travelled to Paris from the United States under the married name of Horus and presented themselves to Mathers as associates of Mme Blavatsky in the American Theosophical Society. Gaining Mathers trust they had somehow procured custody of the most secret rituals and teachings of the Order. At one point Mathers' was said to be credulous of their claim that Madame Horos was the Adept Anna Sprengel with whom his previous co-chief William Westcott had maintained a magical correspondence at the very birth of the Order.

Travelling to London, the couple initiated a money making scheme in the form of a matrimonial agency for respectable young ladies. For some reason, the Horos couple then attempted to use the rituals of the Golden Dawn to induct two vulnerable females who had placed themselves into what appeared to be the formalities of a religious cult. By this time, Mme Horus was passing her husband Theo off as a future world teacher in order to inveigle financial donations from the life-savings of whomsoever they might dupe. The Horus couple were accompanied everywhere by an ageing American heiress who had already parted with a sizable slice of her fortune to the couple and who seemed to be under the hypnotic command of Madame Horus. Things took a turn for the worse after Theo attempted to employ a rite from the Golden Dawn litany in a 'secret marriage' ritual with one of the girls who had answered the couple's matrimonial ads.

The girl's relatives were not impressed to hear that the sacred vows had been exchanged under Theo's bed sheets and involved a lot of esoteric mumbo-jumbo. The police were even less impressed.

By the time of the Horus' trial, the daily newspapers had reduced the Golden Dawn to little more than a public laughing stock on their front pages. Only a handful of rural temples led by J. W. Brodie Innes within the Golden Dawn movement continued to follow the rule of Mathers. The London Lodge decamped under a schismatic continuing fragmentation - at times steered by W.B. Yeats and at others by A.E. Waite before disappearing into subcultural semi-obscurity. Historians are still debating the legitimacy of the various lineages claiming authentic succession from the Mother Lodge. For the main, Mathers made Paris the focus of his Golden Dawn operations from this time onwards, until his death of influenza during the great epidemic of 1917.

Whilst all this was brewing in the cauldron of destiny, Aleister Crowley was about to embark upon the most enchanted period of his poetic and magical development. Whilst he chased the setting Sun to arrive many months later in the lands of the Rising Sun, Crowley would experience a personal revolution in both his understanding of himself and of the mystical and magical arts which consumed his aspirations.

2 -The Awakening of the Adept

Aleister Crowley arrived in New York during an intense ten day heat wave. After receiving his initiation into the Adeptus Minor grade of the Golden Dawn order from Mathers in Paris he had been taking his studies in magic seriously, taking every opportunity on the voyage to practice spiritual exercises such as the assumption of god forms and astral tattwa visions taught in the order syllabus.

Any thought of further magic was scotched by the sweltering heat of the concrete hell of Manhattan and Crowley took to running numerous daily cold baths in a battle against the raging fire of the daytime. Writing about this period he tells us this was his first introduction to real climatic heat. He feared that Mexico, where he intended to do some climbing, might be impossible if a New York heat wave could be so cruel. Advice from friends that this was an aberration gave him some reassurance but after three days Crowley abandoned New York for Mexico via train.

In Mexico the air was pure and dry; the heat not unbearable. At first the young explorer loathed Mexico City. In epicurean terms, Crowley was semi-autistic - attesting to a "fastidious daintiness" in his Confessions, quite at odds with his reputation as a rough and tumble mountaineer and sportsman. He admits to never having tried even a simple salad before the age of forty. With tastes more appreciative of Lobster Brulie, the keen Mexican palate was not to Crowley's liking. The absence of decent champagne, or anything resembling a vintage wine, was also a source of irritation and he refrained from partaking in the delights of Tequila, Mescal and other native liquid ambrosia. In time, Mexico grew on him and Crowley would come to wax lyrical concerning the easy pace of life and the relaxed sexual morality which prevailed; boasting that whatever one's sexual preferences, here one could effortlessly satisfy one's lusts.

During his early period in Mexico the young

magician was still enamored of the teachings of Mathers and the Golden Dawn for he began to practice the order teachings upon attaining Invisibility with some regularity and determination. Sitting in his hotel room and staring into the mirror after a performance of the Golden Dawn banishing rituals, he followed the instructions from the order teaching papers known as 'flying rolls'. These formed a body of teachings to supplement the topics covered in the dramatic initiation and path working rituals.

Following a protracted effort, he managed to make his image in the mirror flicker and momentarily disappear and began to realise that this particular magic depended upon affecting the cognitive consciousness. "But the real secret of invisibility is not concerned with the laws of optics at all; the trick is to prevent people noticing you when they would normally do so. In this I was quite successful. " Satisfied he could replicate this experience, he attempted a number of times to repeat it in public and claimed to have passed in the street unnoticed wearing a golden crown and a scarlet robe. How much of this is actually accounted for by the natural politeness of the Mexican people in overlooking the presence of an exhibitionist

English eccentric amongst them is debatable. Crowley would later pull the same trick in the Cafe Royale, appearing amongst the literati of the day in full wizards robes replete with conical hat and causing a hushed silence to fall. "No one spoke, for no one saw me," he later teased.

Taking on a native girl to look after his daily affairs, Crowley settled down to his routing of magic and correcting the proofs of forthcoming poetic works. By agreeing to fund the printing costs, Crowley was being published in limited runs of 500 hardback editions by Kegan-Paul, gaining favourable notices in a number of periodicals including the London based Occult Review.

Whilst he was acclimatizing to the fresh clear air of Mexico, awaiting the arrival of his climbing companion Eckenstein, the young mystic gained an introduction to a local honorary known as Don Jesus Medina who recruitied him into an unorthodox rite of the 33rd Degree of 'Scottish' Freemasonry. Although this Masonic rite was quite irregular, Crowley felt empowered by his recent Golden Dawn initiation to act with plenipotentiary powers as a Golden Dawn adept to authorize his own secret Order. Thus, in partnership with Don Jesus Medina, the Order of the Ever Burning Lamp was brought into being.

The object of this order was to maintain an ever burning flame which would be continually furnished with the talismans and paraphernalia associated with whichever planets were strongest in the heavens. Crowley describes the initiative as being "with the object of making the light itself a consecrated centre or focus of spiritual energy. This light would then radiate and automatically enlighten such minds as were ready to receive it." Although he refers to this episode in his 'Confessions' he regrets that he lost touch with Don Jesus and never heard anything more of the matter.

On his first expedition out of town, on a hired horse, Crowley discovered a railway line in the process of construction and followed it until night fell "sudden and black". Taking refuge beneath some materials left by the engineers he slept a few hours and awoke as if by instinct to find three heads poked up from behind a sand dune observing him from a distance. He fired his revolver into the air and was not bothered again. The next evening he took refuge with a gang of Chinese railroad workers who scared him with tales of Scorpions falling from the rafters during the night whilst regularly taking care to pour boiling water through the cracks in the floorboards to kill those underfoot. He spent a restless night, though one undisturbed by deadly scorpions. Nevertheless, he awoke in the morning to find his legs so badly swollen by mosquito bites that he could not put on his boots.

Later that day, continuing on horseback he fell in behind a train of pack mules and crossed a hilltop to witness the desiccated corpse of a fallen wayfarer, mummified by the desert sun.

Upon returning to Mexico City, Crowley spent two weeks recovering from Malaria and began to grow disenchanted with the Golden Dawn method of highly dramatized ritual and ceremonial swashbuckling. The young mystic was developing a taste for the psychological arena of esotericism where the personal implications of ritual practice took root in transformations of the underlying spiritual foundations of the identity.

Despite having received his initiation into the grade of Minor Adept, Crowley had still to perform much of the work demanded to take full ownership of the title.   This included the construction of a set of magical tools including the magicians symbols of the four elements, the Pantacle, the chalice, the atheme (dagger) and the wand. For the moment, the aspiring mage was simultaneously coping with keeping himself busy familiarizing himself with the depth of esoteric material which his progress through the four outer grades of Golden Dawn membership had given him exposure.

Fortunately, he had undergone something of a crash course in the magical knowledge covered by the lower four grades whilst living with Alan Bennett. Extensive reading and familiarity with the Greek classics gave him some advantage over the average Golden Dawn aspirant.   His keen and incisive mind easily got to grips with the underlying Qabalistic paradigms of the mystical Tree of Life which the Hermetic school had adopted from Judaic mysticism from the late medieval period.

Crowley's early childhood exposure to a literal reading of the biblical scriptures was also a huge advantage to understanding the underlying theory of magic of the Golden Dawn. Before Mathers sought autocratic authority as sole chief of the order, he shared this honour with Dr

William Westcott who also ran the London lodge of the Theosophical Society for a number of years. Westcott was a biblical scholar and an expert in Chaldean magic who sustained correspondence with colleagues such as Wallace Budge, curator of Egyptian Antiquities at the British Museum and the Theosophist Annie Besant on Rosicrucian matters. It was Westcott who had claimed to be in possession of correspondence from certain Adepts in Germany which authenticated the Golden Dawn's historic chain of ancestry. Recently, Golden Dawn scholars have pointed out that key elements of linguistic German were misconstrued in translation and, although Westcott's translator believed the originator of the letters to be one Anna Sprengel, a genuine correspondence from one of the Germanic Rosicrucian Adepti may actually have been taking place but was misunderstood.

Westcott's biblical scholarship and familiarity with the corpus of medieval post-renaissance hermetic literature helped lay the foundation for the formulation of the grade structure of the Golden Dawn in the image of the ten sephiroth of the Hebrew mystical Tree of Life. The whole Qabalistic schemata of the order was supposedly laid out in a series of cipher manuscripts which Westcott claimed arose from a chance find in an antiquarian book shop. More likely they were papers from the collection of Kenneth McKenzie, an enthusiast of English Magic from an earlier generation who had travelled in Europe widely and even paid court to the French mage Eliphas Levi.

Westcott was a Freemason and introduced a Craft leaning to Golden Dawn rituals. Mathers had trusted Westcott to review his work during his translation of von Rosenroth's Kabbalah Denudata from the Latin and which became his book *The Kabbalah Unveiled*. These texts from the Zohar were reputed to contain the original descriptions of the notional structure of the Tree of Life and many of the Zohar's concepts were adopted into the Golden Dawn's understanding of the mysticism running through the Old Testament.

The 'magic' of the Golden Dawn grade ceremonies was simply the smoke and mirrors of theatrical ceremony. Contained in the speeches of various officers were pointers towards various systems by which the unfolding energies and intelligences of the Creator revealed himself through the geometry of space-time. Printed discourses on these subjects would supplement the student's further understanding, but the real magic of the Golden Dawn lay in the dynamic of the teaching syllabus which called each student to a structured path leading to self-discovery.

Two years into Order membership, Crowley began to discern that the glamour of the ritual pomp distracted from the quality of personal experience. In an intensification of his interior poetic quest, he experimented for the first time with Elizabethan Enochian Magic, based on the evocation of the visions of the Aethyrs, or mystical dimensions, inhabited by the fallen Angels who form the subject of the ancient Book of Enoch.

Originally it was Elizabethan mage Dr John Dee who had spent a number of years documenting mystic interactions with such Angelic forces who systemized the body of magic which came to be known as Enochian. Many think the good Doctor was duped by Edward Kelly, a learned yet criminally minded and manipulative associate who served as his visionary in these angelic matters.

John Dee, a confidante of Queen Elizabeth

herself - he drew up the horoscope to determine the best time for her coronation - left a body of work including hundreds of pages of vast and complex magic squares. Many of these were in a curiously alien symbolic font which constitues the alphabet of the Enochian Angelic language. At the heart of the system are a series of invocations in this strange language which are designed to open the gateway to dimensions of being where visionary experience of the Angelic realm is possible. A crystal was employed as a focus for the experience of these visions.

Mathers had studied Dee's Enochian material and grafted it onto Westcott's Qabalistic grade structure. Even more than this, combining Westcott's knowledge of Indian Four Handed Chess with Mathers' zodiacal correspondences, Egyptian gods and esoteric colour schemes the Golden Dawn even developed a form of divinatory chess based on Dr Dee's Enochian tablets.

This was the magic with which Crowley was determined to get to grips. Despite being only partly familiar with the totality of the Golden Dawn curriculum he attempted to summon visions from the Enochian tablets. As his level of practical commitment to the demands of

Golden Dawn membership had not wavered, being daily engaged upon one mental or meditational exercise or another, he felt himself up to the task. His initial results were encouraging. Describing only a part of his initial visions Crowley describes being cast back in time to the moment of Creation itself:

"Now did I go backwards in time even unto Berashith, the Beginning, and was permitted to see marvelous things.

"First the Abyss of the Water: on which I, even I, brooded amid other dusky flames as Shin upon Maim, held by my Genius. And I beheld the victory of Râ upon Apophis and the First of the Golden Dawns! Yea: and monsters, faces half-formed, arose: but they subsisted not."

Crowley explored two of the Enochian Aethyrs whilst in Mexico, claiming that the Angels he encountered towered over him and looked down upon him in curiosity. Yet, somehow, his success in his magical affairs came too easily to him and subconsciously he must have begun to suspect his own judgment in such matters. He writes:

"In the dry pure air of Mexico, with its spiritual energy unexhausted and uncontaminated as it is in cities, it was astonishingly easy to produce satisfactory results. But my very success somehow disheartened me. I was getting what I thought I wanted and the attainment itself taught me that I wanted something entirely different."

Crowley makes it plain in his Confessions that he had been stunned by Mathers' gullibility in accepting the Horus couple at face value. Returning to Paris immediately prior to his departure for the Americas, to report to Mathers on the latest events in the London Lodge's rebellion against his authority, Crowley had began to suspect his idol may have feet of clay.

Another matter was also troubling him concerning Mathers. After his mountaineering adventures were concluded, he intended to sail to Ceylon to rendezvous with Alan Bennett whose altercation with Mathers over his repeated chanting of the name of Shiva was the subject of much speculation. Bennett was later to confirm that Mathers had pulled a revolver on him in a drunken rage to silence his persistent mantra, being saved by the timely intervention of Mathers' wife Moina.

Feeling disenchanted with Magic, Crowley turned his attention to the mountains which he soon planned to climb with Eckenstein. His young native female servant had called him up to the roof one afternoon and pointed to two snow covered peaks. Such was the clarity of the air that their detail made them appear to be nearby hills. Crowley was surprised that this range was over seventy miles away. These were mountains on an epic scale and he relished the coming challenge.

As he awaited the arrival of Eckenstein, Crowley sought out wretched hags with burning lust in their eyes for sex and to inspire poetic verse. Otherwise he set himself upon the task of examining the numerological system of combining the number value of Hebrew letters, known as Gemetria. Allan had left the notes for an embryonic Qabalistic dictionary in numerological Hebrew in the care of his friend. This work itself had originally been commenced in partnership with Mathers. Now Crowley took himself to generating it into a complete resource which would eventually be published as the work *Sepher Sephiroth*.

At the same time, playing with different combinations of the Hebrew numerology of consonant letters, he discovered a secret cipher rendering alternatives of the original word of magic Abracadabra. These alternatives, the most well-known of which are Abrahadabra and BrHadad, provide a solution to the lost word of the Freemasons. The cult of Hadad was central to the elder Semitic traditions at the time of Abraham when the name of the high God was El, prior to the rise of the cult of IHVH. The title *Had* would be the opening word in his central inspired work, *The Book of the Law*, when it came to be written. In the major commentary he would write upon the Book of the Law which was eventually published as *The Law is for All*, Crowley makes mention of the cult of Hadad in the very first paragraph.

Whilst compiling and further researching 777, Crowley claims in his *Confessions* to have made a series of wonderful gemetria and numerological discoveries. Following a series of instructions he found in Mather's translation of the Zohar to combine the ten sephiroth upon the Qabalistic Tree of Life into the more streamlined form of the ancient system of Seven Palaces, Crowley set to work. By reassigning those letters of the twenty two paths made redundant by the reductive transformation from template of the ten sephiroth to the seven palaces, Crowley worked on the assumption that the 'lost' name of god would reveal itself. In his calculations he believed he had found also the word of the coming Aeon, or era of New Age revelation. Readers are referred to the work *Aleister Crowley's Secret Temple* for further detail upon this area of study.

When Eckenstein arrived for the climbing season in November he found his younger friend unable to contain his enthusiasm about magic, numerology and tales of finding the 'lost' word. Normally Crowley would have kept his esoteric speculations to himself, noting in his autobiography that Eckenstein was very much a no-nonsense man with a taste for a caustic and critical riposte. Perhaps the months of relative solitude weighed heavily upon him but, perhaps for the first time, he was about to receive a lesson in the facts of life.

Unusually, Eckenstein heard Crowley out with some patience before delivering a life changing piece of advice: Crowley must learn to properly concentrate. 'You can't keep one thing in your mind for any length of time without it being chased out by a whole host of genius like thoughts queuing up for the privilege,' he was told. Being confronted with such an outpouring of plain speaking was something of a revelation to Crowley. He had put out a prayer like call to the Masters for assistance only days before this. Could Eckenstein have been the master he was seeking all along? Crowley wondered.

Eckenstein challenged him to build up his Will through the ability to visualize and hold specific items in his mind's eye, setting the younger man a series of mental exercises as challenges. Under Eckenstein's supervision, even whilst their first mountaineering adventure was underway, Crowley would attempt to hold items in mental focus for increasing lengths of time, starting with static objects then onto moving ones. Next he moved on to visualizing humanoid shapes, transferring his consciousness over to them. In a very short time, the young magician realized the fragile disposition of his imaginative will. But he was hooked. Eckenstein's training of the mind exercises seemed to offer better value in terms of results than the arcane methods of the Golden Dawn alone.

Crowley kept up these exercises with regularity and never forgot them. Practicing in the mental realm whilst climbing, Eckenstein sometimes had to pull his companion out of this new habit for interiorizing his mental focus. In later adventures, Crowley would travel by mule and foot across south-western China in a semi-permanent waking trance, as he perfected the mentally envisioned scenarios of whole astral temples. It was the mental training originally encouraged by Eckenstein which provided him with the initial focus and discipline to successfully pull this kind of thing off.

During the couple's first mountain outing they set new world records for speed of ascent and endurance at altitude. Both Eckenstein and Crowley were utilizing the metal climbing 'claws' - spiked boots - which enabled them to attempt ice faces which most climbers of the era would consider impossible. Crowley and Eckenstein were not only setting mountaineering altitude records, they were evolving the methodology of the sport itself. The present adventure in Mexico was intended as preparation for an attempt on the Himalayan peaks the following year. Crowley intended to sail for Ceylon to rendevous with Alan Bennett where he was taking instruction in Yoga from a Shaivite teacher who also happened to be Lieutenant Governor of the Island. He would later rejoin Eckenstein in Northern India for the expedition they had planned.

In the meantime, as they wandered the slopes in the company of T.G. Longstaff, later President of the Alpine Club, they practiced their pistol and rifle marksmanship. Their skill developed to such a degree that they could shoot the bottom out of glass bottles through the neck from some distance away. This impressed the local bandits and kept them from any casual larceny. On one of their journey's they had fallen in with a team of Chinese Engineers who were one short due to their companion having wandered out of the dinner tent for five minutes the evening previously only to be murdered for his suit of clothes, barely worth five shillings in Crowley's estimation.

On their second outing, the adventurers chose a mountain range containing one of the world's most active volcanos which duly erupted as they made their attempt on it. From a range of ten miles, their clothes began to burn with falling cinders. Deciding to proceed during a quiet period in the cycle of eruptions, they eventually retreated from its slopes after finding the soles of their boots melting from the heat of the rock face underfoot. Only after successfully conquering a nearby peak were they were able to look down over the crater of the volcano.

A reporter from the Mexico *Herald* dared to write a report casting doubt over the claims being made for the expedition's achievements. Crowley and Eckenstein were incensed and craftily cornered the writer in his favourite bar there they playfully invited him to accompany them on a climb. Relieved that this might be the full extent of their wrath, the reporter agreed and the next day found himself being prodded up slopes at breakneck speed at the point of Crowley's axe and invited to assail frightening rock faces at pistol point. The next article appearing in the *Herald* to cover the expeditions progress was much more supportive.

Returning from one excursion they heard that Queen Victoria had passed away and surprised their informant by whooping for joy and performing a victory dance. The old Queen had cast a shadow over her Empire since going into permanent mourning after the death of her beloved Albert.

Journeying to Vera Cruz to climb the 18,000 ft Citlatepetl, the team passed through some of the most beautiful sub-alpine gorges Crowley could recall in his later years. Somehow, enthusiasm petered out and Citlatepetl was never attempted. Eckenstein returned to England in April of 1901 and Crowley made haste for San Francisco from where he would sail to Hawaii and thence, via Singapore and Japan, to Ceylon.

Passing through West Texas, he noted in his journal his abhorrence at the stark contrast between the brash culture of the United States and the more relaxed latin romance of Mexico. He also witnessed a man's eyes being gouged out in a casual attack which passed practically uncommented amongst the gathered street peasants. "There are many unpleasant sides of life which cannot be avoided without shirking reality altogether," he wrote, "but in the United States they were naked and horrible. The lust of money raged stark without the softening influences of courtesy. Drunkenness was stripped of good fellowship; the sisterhood of sin presented no deceptive attractions ... All those little grace of life which make bought kisses tolerable to those sensitive people who are willing to be fooled, were absent."

Crowley's diary, recording his arrival in San Fransisco, reports the continuation of the Golden Dawn 'Assumption of Godforms' practices, involving allowing the consciousness of a range of ancient Gods to inhabit one's psyche. It also lists exercises in meditation upon simple symbols and practices for rising on the Astral Planes, seeing in the spirit vision and numerous other entry level ritual observances. He was also continuing the exercises in which Eckenstein had couched him and "got rid of the necessity of the physical temple by expressing it in a series of seven mental operations."

Taking Eckenstein's advice to improve his concentration and focus, Crowley managed to concentrate upon mental images of the Golden Dawn symbols for increasing amounts of time without breaks in attention. Keeping track of his progress with a stop watch and notepad, he recorded one occasion in which he was able to maintain his mental focus for over fourteen minutes.

At this point Crowley also began *Orpheus,* his most epic poetic cycle yet attempted. This was finally completed for publication in 1905. Sailing via Hawaii, Crowley began an affair with a married woman who was traveling with her juvenile son and penned a series of fifty sonnets in the style of Swinburne to celebrate the occasion. These were later published as *Alice: An Adultery.*

Shanghai was hot - the curries hotter. His thoughts in mainland China were of an old girlfriend from his early period of Golden Dawn membership, Elaine Simpson, recently married in Hong Kong to a British Consul. News of her marriage had come as a disappointment to him. He had recently been casually engaged to a rising opera singer he had met whilst attending one of Mathers' public performances of the Mysteries of Isis in Paris 1899: something of a fund and awareness raising exercise on the part of Mathers and his wife. This engagement had fallen through and Crowley had hoped to rekindle the flame from his earlier association with Elaine in the East upon finding himself single again.

Crowley had been maintaining a correspondence with his old flame and even made arrangements to meet her on several occasions upon the astral plane in the spirit body; an ability Crowley maintains he was able to manifest with some skill. Alongside his frustration over the news of Elaine's recent marriage he was disappointed to read in one of her letters that she had won first prize in a Hong

Kong Fancy Dress Party wearing her Golden Dawn robes.

Although Crowley was becoming familiar with the terminology and modus operandi of western hermetic ritual magic, his knowledge of the eastern mysteries to which he was about gain exposure was exceedingly limited. Israel Regardie calls attention to Crowley attempting to summon the 'Angel of Nirvana' as one of the magical exercises he attempted on this voyage. As if such an entity existed!

Spending only a short time stopping over in Japan, where he visited the giant statue of Buddha beneath the open sky at Kamakura, Crowley moved on to meet his old friend and mentor in Colombo, Ceylon.

Crowley was in an expansive mood and grown somewhat more humble and mature from his mountaineering experiences in Mexico and also as a consequence of Eckenstein's mental exercises. Bennett had found himself a job as tutor to the son of Ceylon's lieutenant-governor, the Hon. P. Ramanathan who was also a yogic master of the Hindi Shaivite sect. Under the tutelage of Ramanathan, Bennett became deeply immersed in the practice of Yoga and impressed

Crowley with his solemn dedication. Crowley was keen to learn whatever Alan had to teach him and persuaded his friend to accompany him to Kandy, in the center of the island where they rented a bungalow and practiced Yoga for three months.

His growing disenchantment with Mathers was not eased when Alan confirmed as true the story of his having been threatened by the Golden Dawn chief with a pistol. The pair agreed not to talk about the Golden Dawn and devote themselves daily to Yoga, meditation and Dharana, concentration of the Mind.

The city of Kandy, located in a rising valley whose sides interlace with the surrounding line-geometry of tea plantations, spreads out around a central lake. The scene is one of sun soaked tranquility, quite a contrast to the human jungle of Colombo of which Crowley wrote of with ambivalence: "I love it and loathe it with nicely balanced enthusiasm. Its climate is chronic; its architecture is an unhappy accident; its natives are nasty...."

In June, a copy of The Daily News reached the young poet in Kandy, containing a review of his *The Soul of Osiris* praising him as a 'new mystic' and drily commenting: "If Mr. Crowley and the new mystics think for one moment that an Egyptian desert is more mystic than an English meadow, that a palm tree is more poetic than a Sussex beech, that a broken temple of Osiris is more supernatural than a Baptist Chapel in Brixton, then they are sectarians. . . . But Mr. Crowley is a strong and genuine poet, and we have little doubt that he will work up from his appreciation of the Temple of Osiris to that loftier and wider work of the human imagination, the appreciation of the Brixton Chapel." Crowley was encouraged.

Alan's health was still troubling him and the move to Kandy seemed to stimulate an ease of his condition. Within days of arriving the couple began a strict regime of Yoga, climaxing with a three day period of silence and meditation during which Crowley reached a level of enlightenment whilst mentally reciting the chant 'Aum mi Padmium'.

After weeks of concentration of effort Crowley was nonplussed, despite his recent insights and attainments. Again, success was too easy for him. He writes: "The result of this attainment was what I should least have expected. I was not encouraged to proceed; it seemed as if I had used up the accumulated energy of years. I found it impossible to force myself to continue. It was nearly two years before I resumed any regular practice."

The strict disciplines of Hindu Yoga were effective, but Bennett was now committed to moving on to take up the saffron robe and embrace Buddhism - a philosophy his Golden Dawn brother never became truly enthusiastic about. Crowley was spiritually fully satiated and describing the experience in his recollections wrote, "Dhyana had washed my brain completely out." He described himself as becoming impatient with the whole business.

Although daily yoga continued, it no longer provided their sole focus and Crowley and Bennett took themselves off to visit the ancient cities and temples of the island's interior including the Royal Palace cresting the 200 metre tall rock outcrop of Sigiriya, which eighty years later featured on the magnificent video of the Duran Duran single 'Save a Prayer'. At Anuradapura, Crowley described the ancient world's largest brick dome bell shaped Dagobas as "incomparably greater as monuments than even those of Egypt."

Leaving Bennett to make his way to Burma where he had accepted a position as tutor at a Rangoon Girls' College, Crowley embarked for India initially spending some weeks exploring the southern territories. Here he was surprised to find himself being approached on a train by an elderly gentleman sporting a white beard asking if the younger man needed any assistance, evidently being a newcomer to India. This turned out to be Colonel Olcott of the Theosophical Society. Crowley wrote of this, stating it to be "the first act of kindly thoughtfulness that I had ever known a Theosophist perform --- and the last."

For a while, the explorer roamed the jungle river banks in search of game for his rifle, bagging a number of trophies. He visited the monumental towers of the Temple in Madurai in the Tamil Nadur province which are decorated with thousands of ornate painted statues of the Gods. Crowley describes the interior containing corridor after corridor of majestic sculptures and carved monoliths.

Realizing that certain shrines within the Temple were only available to the natives, he disguised himself as a local tribesman amongst the flocks of pilgrims. No one was fooled by the disguised Englishman with his begging bowl, but he elicited a certain amount of empathy when he demonstrated his knowledge of Yoga. After breaking the ice, he was introduced to the keepers of the vast complex and allowed access to an inner shrine where he was invited to sacrifice a goat. Inspired by his experiences he wrote the poems 'Ascension Day' and Pentecost, which echo his recent Hindu and Buddhist experiences. He also wrote an essay Science & Buddhism, summarizing what he had learned from Bennett which appeared alongside these poems plus an essay on ontology and ceremonial magic in the collection published as *Sword of Song*.

Making a deep study of Hindu religion and mythology Crowley moved on to visit the Temple of Shivalingam in Madras, thence on to Calcutta where he suffered another bout of Malaria.

Bedridden and prescribed quinine and iced champagne, the firebrand adventurer's spirit became a little more placid and he determined to visit Allan in Burma. Having walked out of his new position, Bennett had already taken his vows as a Buddhist Monk at a monastery in

Akyab. Crowley was growing bored of Hinduism and felt like giving Allan's Buddhism another try.

Sailing to Rangoon with a new friend, the artist Edward Thornton, he employed a local as a manservant the trio embarked a five week game-hunt shooting Deer and the occasional Duck. Then, departing Thornton's company, he sailed for Akyab where he was reunited with his spiritual brother Allan Bennett. Catching a cab at the dockside, Crowley discovered his old friend at a bungalow near the Temple, locked in a stiff yoga lotus and tipped on his head, upside down.

After Allan could be prized from his unique posture the pair enjoyed one another's company, spending hours discussing the possibility of introducing Buddhism to the West. Crowley was privately relieved that his friend had found a spiritual home in a climate conducive to his health.

Recovering his own health, Crowley commenced work upon Book III of *Orpheus* and the poetic works *The Argonauts* and *Ahab*. He was only to stay in Akyab for a week before returning to Calcutta where he prepared to rendezvous with Eckenstein and the European team of mountaineers who would accompany him on his attempt on K2 the following Spring and Summer.

On March 23rd Crowley boarded a train to Rawalpindi, where he had agreed to rendezvous with the climbing team only to find Eckenstein and his four associates were fellow passengers. Eckenstein had brought across Cambridge man Guy Knowles, who had helped fund the expedition, two Austrians Pfannl and Wessely - a judge and a barrister - and Jules-Jacot Guillarmod a Swiss physician.

After setting out from Pindi on March 29th with three tons of baggage and over one hundred and fifty porters, the expedition proved itself beset with the first in a long series of difficulties. Crowley woke on the second morning of travel to find a police inspector at the foot of his bed asking for Eckenstein.

As it turned out, the Prussian climber's name had been put forward as a spy and possible murderer and also as an enemy of the British Crown. These were the only 'facts' Crowley was able to later ascertain from rumours on the grapevine. He was to be denied entry into

Kashmir. At the time even the police inspector had no source of real information and the Deputy Governor of the province arrived soon after to escort Eckenstein back to Pindi where he could take the matter up with a higher authority. Crowley became the de facto leader of the expedition in the absence of Eckenstein. They soldiered on.

As the team tramped on across the desolate valleys leading to the Kamakoram mountain range they hired porters wherever they could at ten cents per day. Eckenstein rejoined the expedition in Srinaga and resumed command on the 22nd April. Suspecting that his name had been maligned due to a historic disagreement he had once had with Lord Curzon, current president of the Alpine Club, whose 1892 expedition to this area included the younger Eckenstein. The Prussian was anathema to the Alpine Club who considered his innovations and outspokenness unwelcome. He considered them inferior climbers. Eckenstein had taken the bull by the horns and cabled Curzon in Whitehall. The results were swift and immediate. Suddenly the Governor of the province could not be more helpful and supplied all the necessary permits and extra Sherpas.

Askole, ten days march from the foot of K2, was the nearest supply village and Eckenstein and Crowley realized they would need an extra twenty days of provisions for the whole team, sherpas and all. Investing heavily, they bought up every scrap of food available in the village and hired wagons and 250 local men to haul their reserves to base camp.

The expedition proceeded in four teams. Crowley's team herded fifteen sheep and thirty goats. Trouble was not long in coming as the Northern Indian Sherpas were an unlikely assembly. A whole group of chancers tagged along just behind the ranks only to swell the lines awaiting their wage at the end of every day. Crowley dealt summarily with a troublemaker who chose to run his cart from the pathway into a ditch. Grabbing the man by his beard, a grave insult by local standards, he commenced to thrash him with a leather belt in order to set an object lesson in respect.

Crowley and Eckenstein temporarily fell out over the formers insistence that he bring along his library of hand-bound red vellum editions of poetry and esoteric classics. Crowley had insisted upon laying in over eighty pounds of extra sugar, but much got sold by rogue Sherpas to villagers along the way causing a case of severe sugar starvation in the later stages of the expedition.

After a seventy nine day march from Pindar they reached the foot of K2 which loomed eight thousand feet over the plateau, filling the sky like a colossal snow covered pyramid.

Over the next sixty eight days, making several camps, the team reached altitudes of over twenty thousand feet and set new endurance records for altitude. Of these nine weeks and five days, Crowley reports only eight days of clear weather. Mountaineers of the successful oxygen-assisted later attempt upon the summit in 1954 complained bitterly about fourteen days of bad weather. K2 is the second highest mountain in the world and the most dangerous to climb. As recently as August 1st 2008 eleven summit climbers lost their lives in a single day.

For the Eckenstein-Crowley expedition to have survived sixty eight days on the ice faces in such abominable weather was a remarkable feat. Crowley suffered snow blindness, malaria and a fever from a liver chill. Eckenstein was confined to the lower camps after falling ill with altitude sickness. Knowles and the Dr Guillarmod came down with influenza. Mountaineers who followed in their wake describe similar storms in grim terms and note the psychologically debilitating effect of prolonged isolation in an exposed canvas tent whose walls are noisily banging in near hurricane force winds.

According to Crowley's account, only the Doctor and himself did not lose their wits at some point during the ascent. The two Austrians Pfannl and Wessely were committed at the outset to making heroic attempts. They requested three days supplies and a chance of first crack at the ascent, which was denied after due consideration. They persisted in making nuisances of themselves and used up all their available energy by the end of July, with Pfannl falling so ill that Wessely was forced to return with him to the lower camps.

According to Crowley: "Pfannl was suffering from oedema of both lungs and his mind was gone." Five days after this the remaining team discovered that the Austrians had taken nearly all the teams emergency food reserves with them. When the climbers eventually did return to the foot of the mountain they were incensed with anger to find that the Austrians had also slaughtered and eaten the greater part of the number of goats and sheep the expedition had arrived with. Dr Guillarmod was noted by the Sherpas as a source of amusement. He was regularly getting into amateurish scrapes on the mountainside, even leaving his Sherpa in a gulley on one occasion, prompting a rescue by Crowley and Eckenstein.

Only Knowles, the least experienced mountaineer, survived the expedition with any credit. In his later years he became a professional collector of fine art and, amongst the exhibits above his fireplace, he kept a pistol which Crowley, driven by fever to paranoia, had threatened him with in a tent on the windswept slopes of K2.

The storm which had been raging since Pfannl and Wesserly had abandoned their reconnaissance of the approach to the Summit intensified on the day Crowley discovered the Austrian's raid upon the emergency rations. On the seventh day, it was agreed to abandon the expedition and the four remaining climbers made their way down the ice face, camp by camp, in the face of a bitter and unrelenting Himalayan storm. As they reached Camp 7, Crowley comments that "the high peaks were 'smoking their pipes', indicating intense winds at the summits causing columns of ice and snow to sweep through the heights."

For the return journey from the mountain the expedition split into two teams. Eckenstein's team retraced their steps and made the return journey through an almost alien landscape of eccentric rock formations and thence across torturous ravines. Crowley took a path demanding that he ford several major rivers to reach Srinagar.

Back in India, taking over a month to recuperate from exhaustion and Malarial fever, most of which time he spent shooting bears, he set sail for the West to reach Aden, Egypt on October 9th. By the 14th of the month he was ensconced in Shephards Hotel, Cairo and preparing himself for the fleshpots of Cairo.

When Crowley arrived in Egypt the Boulaq Museum had been closed for nearly three years according to the author Richard T Cole. Writing in his *Liber vel Bogus: The Real Confessions of Aleister Crowley*, Cole suggests that the magician could not have come into contact with the Stele of Boulak (sic), a colorfully decorated wooden funerary stele, earlier than 1905 – on a trip to Cairo he does not mention in his Confessions.

This artefact was inscribed with texts from The Book of the Dead for the occasion of the death of a Theban priest Ankh af na Khonsu and depicts the goddess Nuit arched over the figure of Ankh af na Khonsu and Ra Hoor Khuit - a form of Horus - beneath a winged disc.

When Crowley returned to Cairo in 1904 with his new wife Rose, he would perform a series of rituals based upon imagery found upon this ancient item in the weeks prior to the experience of receiving The Book of the Law. In all his writings Crowley claims that his wife discovered the Stele in 1904 in the Boulaq Museum as exhibit 666. As the Boulaq had been closed for three years by that point, it may be that the exhibit was shown as part of the Boulaq Collection at Cairo Museum and that Crowley is misremembering. Richard Cole posits an armful of inconsistencies in Crowley's published accounts of the episode and also raises the possibility that Crowley took notice of this in a catalogue during his earlier visit to the country.

In his autobiography the mage recounts that he

was growing more realistic about Magic and still feeling a little disenchanted with Mathers. In spite of this, for the meantime he was charitable enough to extend some faith in Mathers' past experience in bringing about the rise of the Golden Dawn and give him the benefit of the doubt. Crowley was still paying semi-regular attention to performing his Golden Dawn exercises, as he had during his mountaineering expeditions, but had a mind to enjoying the materialistic benefits of the West after his deprivations in the East.

3 - Towards the Silver Star

The glories of Egypt were not enough to hold Crowley's attention. He wrote: "I lived at Shephards' Hotel till Guy Fawkes's Day, wallowing in the flesh pots. I would not even go out to see the Pyramids. I wasn't going to have forty centuries look down on me."

Returning to Paris Crowley hooked up with his old college friend Gerald Kelly, who introduced him to the Artist and Sculptor Rodin.

He also called on Mathers and found the Golden Dawn chief affectedly uninterested in his oriental exploits or mountaineering adventures.

Mathers had lost possession of a fifty guinea dressing case which Crowley had left in his care before embarking on his circumnavigation of the globe. He began to suspect the older man had fallen prey to the negative forces of the Abramelin operation and sold the item for whisky and pocket money. Remaining charitable to Mathers in such circumstances demonstrates something of Crowley's nobility of character, for the returning adventurer remained on relatively good terms with the Golden Dawn master, even though his disillusionment was rising.

The social scene in the French capital was bustling with Artists and Writers. Crowley met Arnold Bennett, famous for his portrayal of life in the Potteries in his Clayhanger novels, was amazed to be accorded with the greatest respect in France due to having had his written work published. Art and high culture were important to the French and they lionized their own literary greats. Paul Bartlett, whose work adorns the portico above the American Senate building, was another acquaintance whom the young poet rubbed shoulders with at the Chat Blanc in the rue d'Odess where the great and the good wined and dined. Here Crowley came to the attention of the writer Somerset-Maugham who made him the protagonist in his novel *The Magician.*

After being taken along to Rodin's studio by Gerald Kelly Crowley met the Sculptor who, at the time, was facing the reaction of influential critics to his sculpture of Balzaac. As he had with Mathers, Crowley offered to place his fortune at the disposal of the Master and wrote sonnets inspired by his works which were published in 1907 as *Rodin in Rhyme.*

Returning to his Scottish lair on the shores of Loch Ness in May 1903, Crowley resumed the preparatory magical exercises for the Abramelin work. This was a traditional six month long magical ritual designed to put him in touch with his Holy Guardian Angel, which he had abandoned some twelve months previously. In early June, he moved his bed into the room which had been set aside as temple space for the operation and experienced frighteningly vivid nightmares of Abramelin demons. These are forces of opposition determined to distract the magician from the essential inner purity required to achieve a state of mystic communication with the Guardian Angel entity. In later stages of the ritual procedure a light powder is scattered over the ground in order to record the footprints of the semi astral entities of Abramelin magic. By mid-June he resumed yoga practices as a means of self-purification, which continued for the next six weeks

In mid-July Crowley was replenishing his wine cellar in Edinburgh and met up with Gerald Kelly who was traveling with his mother and younger sister Rose, later to become Crowley's first wife. Crowley played a game of golf with Kelly who brought along his sister. Rose had a complicated love life and was engaged to be married although finding herself in love with another man altogether. Crowley describes her as highly intelligent but uneducated and of high spirits. In later writings he tells a story of how she had shocked her parents by revealing a pregnancy which they provided funds to terminate. In actuality there was no pregnancy and the only expenditure was on dinners and frocks. The pair got along famously.

Rose's matrimonial predicament was urgent. She was only weeks away from marrying an unpleasant suitor and beginning to panic; confiding all this to Crowley in a private moment. In a demonstration of cavalier lateral-thinking he offered to wed her in a 'name only' marriage, which would free her from the pressure of suitors and family alike. The romanticism of the gesture appealed to them both and they secretly eloped, marrying in Dingwall, Scotland on August 12th in the office of the local sheriff. Rose's brother Gerald narrowly missed interrupting the marriage, having been in hot pursuit since finding his sister missing from her chambers. He burst in only minutes after the ceremony ended and threw a comical mis-aimed punch at his new brother in law.

The bride returned to her family and the groom to Boleskine House, intending to remain true to the 'name only' marriage. This noble ideal soon fell sacrifice to the pragmatism which circumstances demanded and Crowley was summoned by his new mother in law to take responsibility for his actions. Rose was willing, even eager, to go along with this and Gerald was pacified.

Crowley had been expecting a red haired housekeeper from Edinburgh to warm his bed. His houseguest Duncombe Jewel, an old friend of the Crowley family and general rake 'on the lam' from mounting debts and a pregnant lover, was dispatched to the city to head her off.

The married couple now did the unthinkable and fell in love. Crowley was later to describe his honeymoon as one long sexual debauch. Rose took an interest in his Magick and the poet found himself once again inspired to write great poetry for his Muse:

"Rose on the breast of the world of spring, ...
I press my breast against thy bloom;
My subtle life drawn out to thee; to thee
....its moods and meaning cling.
I pass from change and thought to peace,
....woven on love's incredible loom,
Rose on the breast of the world of spring."

The newlyweds were soon to embark on a glittering Honeymoon, intending to take in big game hunting in Ceylon, visiting Allan Bennett in Burma and thence on to China - taking in Egypt on the way. Hopping across the English Channel and stopping over in Paris the couple chanced upon Mrs Moina Mathers on the street, who Crowley described as "painted to the eyes." In his Confessions he repeats the rumour that Mathers had encouraged his wife to display as a nude model in one of the popular Montmartre shows having fallen on hard times. Crowley was so shocked, he forgot to introduce his wife who assumed Mrs Mathers to have been a model of his previous acquaintance.

From Paris a train bore them to the south coast where they alighted a steamer for Egypt. Together they spent an evening in the Kings Chamber of the Great Pyramid where Crowley raised an astral light. He describes this to have been as bright as tropical moonlight engendered by reading out the Preliminary Invocation of the Goetia, from Mathers' translation of the work by candlelight. After an uncomfortable night on the stone floor of the chamber the astral light had dissipated and the only sound was the flitting of bats.

Proceeding to Ceylon, Rose found herself pregnant and after only a matter of a few short weeks on the island they boarded a boat heading west so that Rose could be delivered of the baby in the safety of the British Isles. In the brief few weeks of January 1904 which they spent in Ceylon, Crowley hunted Stag and Elephant accompanied by his wife and a team of trackers. They made camp near a beautiful lake whose banks bordered on marshland and which was surrounded by magnificent jungle. The trees were full of flying foxes and the sky full of bats. Somehow one of these creatures fell and attached itself to Rose with its claws, causing considerable consternation. That night Crowley awoke to the cry of a dying bat to find his wife absent from the bed. Arising he found her naked, clinging to the tent frame "with arms and legs, insanely yawling." He reported it was the finest case of obsession he had ever seen.

On January 28th, the couple sailed for Aden and thence Port Said where they alighted to arrive in Cairo on February 8th. On the voyage Crowley had fallen into conversation with Dr. Henry Maudsley, a leading academic philosopher of the era, with whom he discussed the mechanistic and physiological model of consciousness. Maudsley was an embryonic advocate of the cognitive school of psychology, which examines innate physiological based capabilities of mental experience. The parameters of the conversation included states of yoga meditation such as Samadhi and Crowley gives a flavour of this interchange of ideas as evidence of his 'skeptical-rationalistic' mode of thought at the time:

"We can produce fantastic dreams by hashish, hallucinations of colour by Anhalonium

Lewinii; we can even make him "see stars" by the use of a sandbag. Why then should we not be able to devise some pharmaceutical, electrical or surgical method of inducing Samadhi; create genius as imply as we do other kinds of specific excitement? Morphine makes men holy and happy in a negative way; why should there not be some drug which will produce the positive equivalent?"

In his autobiography, Crowley admits that in considering this line of thinking "the mystic gasps with horror, but we really can't worry about him."

His experiences during the next few weeks were about to change his life forever and provide a reference point which he would revisit in his writings for the next four decades. In typical style Crowley announced himself in Cairo as Prince Chioa Khan, the Hebrew name for Beast, disguised as an eastern prince in turban and costly jewels. After a leisurely month playing golf and visiting the museums, the couple moved into a flat in Cairo where Crowley repeated the invocation from The Goetia, wanting to summon the elemental spirits of Air known as Sylphs, for Rose to enjoy. Instead, she fell into a trance and began to repeat the words: "They are waiting for you." The next day, he made more invocations and Rose repeated her response adding: "It's all about the child" and "All Osiris."

Ignoring any implication that this message from the gods could in any way be linked to the birth of his coming child, a thought which may have crossed the mind of any lesser mortal, Crowley invoked the Egyptian god Thoth later that day. The results were encouraging.

The next day, Rose revealed that "the waiter" was Horus, the child god of the Egyptian pantheon, "whom I had offended and ought to invoke." Crowley surmised that this was "the child" to whom Rose had originally referred. He began to question her, asking her to describe the god to ascertain the veracity of her vision and her answers were sufficiently detailed to satisfy his skepticism.

As Rose's trance deepened, she imparted instruction to her husband on how to invoke Horus. From the point of view of Crowley's Golden Dawn training the instructions made little sense and he describes them as "rubbish." The next day, the 19th March, he carried out her instructions to the letter in order to demonstrate that little would happen if they deliberately broke the rules of magic. In full ceremonial robes, Crowley performed the invocation provided by Rose at the stroke of Noon before an open window looking out onto a busy Cairo street. Nothing happened. He suggested to his wife that he try again at midnight, whereupon he reported astonishing success in the operation. A disembodied voice informed him from the darkness that "The Equinox of the Gods had come" and instructing him to forge a link between mankind and the spiritual solar-force about to launch itself in a new Aeon or astrological age.

All this was music to Crowley's ears. For some time now the coming of the new World Teacher had been prophesied by Blavatsky's Theosophical Society and writers such as Alice Bailey. A number of Crowley's earlier works had self-referenced the poet as an agent sent to prepare the way for a new age of free-thinking. He knew that Annie Besant, the current leader of the Theosophical Society, would be a passenger on the steamer back to Europe on which they intended to return at the close of March. It must surely have crossed his mind to use this opportunity to announce himself?

At the same time, Crowley was more or less completely disenchanted with Golden Dawn leader Macgregor Mathers. Thoughts of displacing his former chief and assuming the mantle of chief of the order were prominent in his mind. His recent magical successes confirmed to the young pretender that he was now in touch with the kind of authentic 'hidden Masters' whom Mathers claimed to have met in Paris.

Amusingly enough, Annie Besant was returning from a visit to the Indian headquarters of the Theosophical Society where the dust was still settling from the scandal surrounding the communications of their own 'hidden masters'. Madame Blavastky had claimed to have been in communication with a school of discarnate intelligences, the principle of whom - Koot Hoomi - was inclined to write letters to her on modern paper in Indian Ink. Following a wide exchange of written chit-chat, which would spontaneously appear in a wooden cabinet, an investigation by Franz Hartmann and the Society for Psychical Research revealed a concealed panel in the woodwork. Evidence of possible sleight of hand had caused an uproar amongst the membership, who still clamored for any genuine evidence of the existence of Theosophy's secret brotherhood.

The period following Crowley and Rose's success at invoking Horus is shrouded in a growing mystery. In his retrospective writings Crowley reports dragging Rose around the Boulaq Museum and asking her to identify the god. According to his reports, she pointed towards a large wooden funerary stelé which displays a long dead Theban Priest - Ankh af na Khonsu - making supplication to the war god Ra-Hoor-Khuit. Crowley recognized this as a manifestation of Horus in his warrior guise and commissioned a translation of the Egyptian Hieroglyphs decorating the monument.

In his *Confessions*, Crowley notes of this period: "The point is that the events of March and April were not in the normal course of the life of a consistent mystic and magician. There was no tendency on my part to accept "divine" interference in my affairs. There was, on the contrary, the bitterest opposition from me. I even went so far as to make unintelligible and false additions to my diary, with the deliberate intention of confusing the record, and perhaps even of making people think me untrustworthy in this stupendous circumstance." This is a strange and ominous admission.

Richard T Cole, writing in his *Liber vel Bogus: The Real Confessions of Aleister Crowley*, notes the fact that the museum where Rose and Crowley made this discovery had been closed for around eighteen months at the time of their reported visit. Cole also notes that Crowley's later reports of the magical work with Rose around the time of their invocation of Horus are also curiously absent from his handwritten journals of the time - including his supposed 'cross examination' of Rose as to the identity of Horus. Israel Regardie, an early biographer of the Beast, also describes strange marks and ciphers in Crowley's diaries of the time. It seems that he was eager to conceal his daily dealings.

During this period the magician was keen to explore the rudiments of mystical Islam and studied the roots of the system under a Sufi Sheikh. He writes: "From this man I learnt also many of the secrets of the Sidi Aissawa; how to run a stiletto through one's cheek without drawing blood, lick red hot swords, eat live scorpions, etc."

Perhaps the secrets of Sidi Aissawa were not far

from his mind on April 8th, when the scribe took up his pen and opened himself to the voice of inspiration whilst he engaged in a feat of automatic writing.   On this date, according to his own report, Crowley began three daily one hour operations of magic which resulted in him penning Liber L vel Legis, The Book of the Law at the behest of an unseen 'minister of the gods' of ancient Egypt who announced himself as Aiwass; Crowley's own Guardian Angel.

The three chapters of The Book of the Law, received on successive days according to its earthly scribe, were to form the central pillar of Crowley's writings, practices and teachings in the latter half of his life. As a piece of prose poetry alone the work is unique enough, containing passages of astonishing beauty and sublime imagery.   The letters of the original Latinate name of the book, 'Liber L vel Legis' all add to 666 when considered in Hebrew numerical equivalents.   Later, the work of Charles Stansfield Jones, Frater Achad, would reveal the term AL to be one of the keys to the work and Crowley changed the title to Liber Al vel Legis, in preference to Liber L vel Legis, needlessly ruining the numerology of the original - of which he was, surprisingly enough, apparently unaware. He certainly never made reference to this in any of his published works.

Within the text of the Book of the Law lies the philosophy of Thelema, Greek for Will, which can be best summed up by its central axiom 'Do what Thou Wilt'. According to Crowley, this had equivalence with the Delphic Oracle's 'Man - Know Thyself': the challenge of finding one's True Will and determining to express it. This, he assures us, takes care of the matter of life's purpose.

The language of the Book of the Law is transcendent:

"Had! The manifestation of Nuit.

The unveiling of the company of heaven.

Every man and every woman is a star.

Every number is infinite; there is no difference.

Help me, o warrior lord of Thebes, in my unveiling before the Children of men!

Be thou Hadit, my secret centre, my heart & my tongue!

Behold! it is revealed by Aiwass the minister of Hoor-paar-kraat.

Steven Ashe

The Khabs is in the Khu, not the Khu in the Khabs.

Worship then the Khabs, and behold my light shed over you!

Let my servants be few & secret: they shall rule the many & the known.

These are fools that men adore; both their Gods & their men are fools.

Come forth, o children, under the stars, & take your fill of love!

I am above you and in you. My ecstasy is in yours. My joy is to see your joy."

Crowley considered himself the awaited World Teacher at this point - in metaphysical terms he embodied the Logos, or Word of the Aeon. In the preceding age of Osiris, the paternal gods had predominated. The era of the Christianity and the Abrahamic religions were at an end. The word of Jesus, Agapé (Love) was superseded by Crowley's pronouncement of Thelema (Will)..

One statement in Liber Al completely knocked all thoughts of pursuing the path of Buddhism from Crowley's head: *"Remember all ye that existence is pure joy; that all the sorrows are but as shadows; they pass & are done; but there is that which remains."*

Towards the later period of his life, Crowley would address all who met him with a pronouncement from The Book of the Law: *"Do what thou wilt shall be the whole of the Law."* The expected response to this would be: *"Love is the Law. Love under Will,"* another quotation from Liber Al ... or Liber L, as it was originally titled.

Crowley later claimed that he mislaid the manuscript of this work for a period of five years until it allegedly turned up again in 1909 in the attic of his Scottish mansion. When it did, it had miraculously reappeared on typing paper bearing a watermark which identified it as a manufactured product of 1905 - nearly nine months after Crowley reports the genesis of the work. This has brought his account of the *Book of the Law's* origin into question. Even amongst Crowley acolytes, this event in the history of Thelema is referred to as the 'reception myth'. By the time he had reached old age, the mage had offered a series of alternate remembering of the events of that time, none of which were in complete agreement with contemporary diary entries.

As he commissioned two typescripts of Liber Al in Cairo, immediately after the writing of the manuscript, any work he did on the text prior to 1909 was in reference to these. Reportedly, both typescripts contain errors and deviations from the manuscript. It must have been from these which Crowley prepared the version he intended to publish as an Appendix to his 1905 *Collected Works* as an example of Automatic Writing at its finest as he described the piece. This never saw the light of publication, however the proofs for these appendices still exist and have been published on the world wide web.

The index subtitle which Crowley ascribes to the typescript of The Book of the Law is Liber 220, which is the number of verses in the text and also the number of times the letter k appears in the original. Recently, those making claims to Crowley copyrights have altered a single letter of the text of the Book of the Law rendering the word Fill to Kill - thus completely altering the original text as Crowley preferred to have it printed. This decision was made without even a footnote to the printed text and appears to have been made on the basis of a penciled note appearing in a copy which Crowley gave away to James Thomas Windram. This was a gentleman whom Crowley had relieved of a sizeable amount of money in exchange for esoteric certificates and meaningless Masonic titles including the right to represent the OTO, a pseudo Freemasonic Degree mill, in the continent of Africa. On the many online chat boards, where the subject is discussed, the Windram copy is sometimes referred to as the 'Windram Edition', which misleadingly leads readers to assume that a whole print edition of the volume is at issue rather than a single hand annotated copy.

The manuscript text purported to be the original was published under the subtitle Liber 31 - the value of AL in Hebrew - after he had extended the title to Liber AL vel Legis in later years.

Numerology plays a major key in the magical fabric of Liber Al and the Book of the Law is full of cryptograms and veiled illusions to obscure Golden Dawn symbols and lore. At one point in the text there is a reference to the number 718 which mystifies many non Qabalists. Upon the Tree of Life diagram which lies at the core of Qabalistic teaching the ten sephiroth are connected by twenty two paths represented by Hebrew letters. Each of these letters has an equivalent numeric integer - a fact which provides Hebrew words with mathematical values. In the Golden Dawn school this diagram is reproduced with the symbol of a serpent winding its body from top to bottom, touching certain paths as it descends. When one adds together the numerology value of each of the Hebrew letter-paths which the serpent does not touch, the sum adds to 718.

Crowley himself regarded the Book of the Law as a work of cryptography. Writing in his Equinox of the Gods, he states: "...no forger could have prepared so complex a set of numerical and literal puzzles."

However much we choose to believe or dispute the reception myth of *Thelema*, Crowley's new toolbox for Mankind's metaphysical ills has evolved to take its place amongst Neo-Futurist philosophies propelling its own share of contemporary cults. Adherents of Crowley's vision for the spiritual future of mankind are a varied lot. Alongside intellectual students of the phenomenon a number of cultists, psychedelic visionaries, tantric enthusiasts and general Anti-Christians appear to represent the majority of The Beast's disciples. In addition to these a small core of self dedicated students of *Thelema* investigate the historic threads behind Crowley's vision and incorporate Graco-Egyptian teachings, ancient Near East temple design, the comedy of Dante and Rabelais and the allegory of the Hermetic Texts into their studies. In all, a varied lot and quite removed from the expected cartoon Satanists which Evangelical Christian paranoia tends to worry over.

It is important to note that Crowley had reached a point in his magical studies following his Adeptus Minor initiation ceremony under Mathers in Paris. In this Golden Dawn ritual Crowley would have taken the oath of the Adeptus Minor pending evidence of the mastership of this grade. The reception of the Book of the Law provided Crowley with this evidence of this attainment, or so he deemed. Soon afterwards he wrote to Mathers in Paris declaring himself to be *de facto* leader of the Order.

In progressive accounts which Crowley reports of this period in Cairo, the reports grow increasingly grandiose and more mystical as time progresses. At first, Crowley was confident enough to pass the piece off as an effective product of 'automatic writing', a poetically inspired process of revelation. He states as much in the title of an intended appendix to his 1905-1907 volumes of *Collected Works*. By the time Crowley was collaborating with Golden Dawn mentor George Cecil Jones upon the founding of a new magical order - the A.'. A.'. a few years later, Liber Legis had been promoted to the status of a Holy Text for the coming Age.

Richard T. Cole dares to discuss the probability that the main episode of events in Cairo previously reported as historic fact are inventions constructed retrospectively, at different times and for a variety of reasons. And amidst the passages of speculation and informed conjecture, the evidence Mr Cole presents is pretty damning.

In his Liber L vel Bogus: The Real Confessions of Aleister Crowley, the author demonstrates a number of disparities in Crowley's unfolding account of the events of this period. Missing pages of diary entries for the period concerned seems the least of the inconsistencies Crowley apologists need to find answers for. The matter of the watermarked typing copy paper, which was only available from 1905 onward, which provided the substrate of the 'original manuscript' of the 1904 document is a matter which might concern those seeking the truth of the matter. But these are only two of the many examples of the unreliability of the evidence supporting the view of events presented by Crowley over the years.

Early in his book, Richard T Cole discusses Crowley's psychological state, stating that a conservative appraisal of his autobiographical confessions would award him 38/40 on Robert D Hare's Psychopathy Checklist. The author points out that, over thirty years after the event, when discussing his 'Confessions' with Jackson Burke in 1938, taped for a later broadcast by a San Francisco radio station, Crowley is still bragging about raping a servant girl at knife-point: obtaining an alibi at the tobacconists to avoid retribution. He proudly notes the girl's genuine accusations were disbelieved against the word of a young gentleman and she was cast out onto the street and made homeless for her 'lies', later dying a paupers death after turning to Prostitution. Mr Cole makes mention of the instance of a young Crowley torturing a cat to death in nine different ways to explore the popular myth of its having nine lives. The shadow of psychopathy cannot be far from the mind of the critical reader.

At the root of this callous pathology, Mr Cole suggest the incident of the accident with fireworks and two pounds of gunpowder which put the lad of sixteen in a coma for ninety six hours and most likely damaged his brain's pre-frontal lobes leaving him with the moral responses normally associated with those of a psychopath or sociopath. Colin Wilson, writing in *The Occult*, cites the same teenage accident with gunpowder and draws the conclusion that it may be this near death experience which ignited Crowley's quest for things magical.

Leaving Egypt from Port Said, Crowley met Annie Besant but did not announce himself as World Teacher.

Returning to Boleskine House in Scotland via Paris, where he and Rose dined with the writer Arnold Bennett, Crowley packed his copies of Liber Legis in a box in the attic and returned to magic. As Spring turned to Summer he published Mathers' translation of The Goetia as 'The Lesser Key of Solomon' for which he wrote an introduction.

Crowley and Rose began experimenting with

sexual aspects of ritual, incorporating sex and sodomy, based upon the symbolism of the Egyptian Stelé which had inspired Rose and led Crowley to pen the Book of the Law. Before leaving Egypt, he had commissioned one of the artists working at the Cairo museum to reproduce an exact copy of the artefact. The magician's journals of the time record a ritual where Rose was expected to maintain a ritual position with "arse as high as possible." It seems that this era marks the period in which Crowley began to work seriously with sexual dynamics in his magical rituals. There is certainly evidence of sexual symbolism related to magic in the pages of the three volume collection of his literary works which Crowley began to publish the following year. These facts tend to contradict the commonly held belief that he was introduced to sexual magic techniques only after he was invited to join the OTO around 1912.

In magical terms, Crowley was no longer in a position to continue his attempt to complete the Abramelin operation. The astral environment had grown hostile. His pack of Bloodhounds mysteriously fell ill and died. He believed Mathers was waging war on the astral plane and responded by performing a ritual magic summoning of Be'elzebub (Ba'al) and his 49 Servitors. Rose developed clairvoyance began to experience visions of ectoplasmic jelly-fish, the figure of a monstrous dwarf and a giant pink bug floating through the air.

The grounds at Boleskine became infested with a peculiar type of Beetle. Crowley equated this with ominous words from the third chapter of The Book of the Law which read: ".... it shall become full of beetles as it were and creeping things sacred unto me."

In July, Rose gave birth to a daughter which they christened Nuit Ma Ahathoor Hecate Sappho Jezebel Lilith. Rose's family were not impressed. Crowley wrote pornography for his wife during her convalescence and played a number of practical jokes on the locals. These included erecting a sign leading to the hills which read "This way to the Kooloomooloomavlock (does not bite)". Locals began to fear this embryonic Loch Ness Monster. He also wrote to a local paper using a pseudonym stating that prostitution was conspicuous in the nearby village of Foyers. After an investigation, the authorities publicly denied this was the case. Crowley wrote back:

"Conspicuous by its absence, you fools."

After a November break on the continent visiting St Moritz, Crowley and Rose returned to Boleskine to entertain Dr Jacot Guillarmod, hoping to interest Crowley in a second Himalayan climbing adventure. This time, the target peak would be Kangchenunga, the world's third highest mountain and at that time unconquered.

No expert on Scottish culture, particularly the Scottish sense of humour, Dr Guillarmod soon fell foul of one of is host's very finest pranks. Crowley "... thought it plausible to invent a wild sheep on the analogy of the wild buffalo. And more, the beast should be already famous. I described its rarity, its shyness, its ferocity, etc., etc. --- "You have doubtless heard of it," I ended; "it is called the haggis."

Crowley's manservant came crashing into the dining room one evening to breathlessly report a rare appearance of the wild beast on the moors. Guillarmod was issued with an Elephant Gun and dragged through the garden fish pond 'to throw off the scent' before being led through the fog to blow apart a recently tethered prize ram with his overwhelming ordinance.

Crowley agreed to provide major funding for the Kangchenunga expedition if the others agreed to sign a contract naming him the leader of the expedition whose judgment should not be questioned.   His   climbing   companion Eckenstein who had led the K2 attempt had elected to steer clear of this venture, believing Guillarmod's "vanity, inexperience, fatuity and folly were certain to land us in disaster" as Crowley put it.

In May Crowley left England on the P & O line cruse ship Marmora and made rendezvous with Guillarmod in Darjeeling.   On July 31st the team of mountaineers set off for Kanchenjunga. This team comprised of Alexis Pache and Charles-Adolphe Reymond whom Guillarmod had recruited and a young Hotel Manager whom had struck Crowley as a competent logician, Rigo de Righi.

Despite Crowley and Eckenstein's criticism of the Jules Jacot Guillarmod's climbing prowess, he was a competent topographer and surveyed the landscape around Kanchenjunga with a Vérascope, one of the first commercially available stereoscopic cameras.   Images obtained using this device allowed the Doctor's cousin Charles Jacot Guillarmod to compile historically acclaimed early maps of the Himalayan region. In all other aspects, this historic attempt to climb one of the world's tallest peaks without oxygen ended in unmitigated disaster - some losing their lives, Crowley his reputation.

Whatever occurred on the slopes of Kangchenjunga, the mountain of the five sacred peaks, the team spirit had fallen apart by the time Camp IV had been established within sight of elevations which would see the team beat world altitude records. Surviving team members blamed the breaking of morale on Crowley's aggressive attitude to the Sherpas, which led him to coax the barefoot natives to greater heights and exertions at the point of his ice axe. Their leader was also reportedly incensed by minor breaks in the agreement for climbing schedules and highly critical of his peers. For his part, Crowley denies the charges of cruelty to the porters, attributing it to the imagination of Guillarmod who had failed to gain the porter's respect in the same way he had succeeded in and whom consequently could not get the men to obey him.

Alexis Pache, who eventually died on the

slopes, accused Righi of withholding food from them on the higher camps through mismanagement. Crowley went so far as to accuse the incompetent supply officer of criminal negligence, for the situation was life threatening at such altitudes. Sending word down to Guillarmod to ensure that supplies were sent up immediately Crowley was the next morning amazed to behold Guillarmod ascending with his fellow climbers and twenty porters, none carrying supplies or shelter - even for themselves.

As it turned out, mutiny was afoot. Guillarmod dismissed the contract naming Crowley as expedition leader as "just a piece of paper" and called a meeting in which Crowley was voted down as chief. He was stunned. Particularly so when it turned out that Guillarmod intended to make a night time descent to Camp IV and that Pache, who should have known better, decided to join them. Crowley warned them that they faced certain death and advised that their decision placed them beyond aid. He gave clear indication that they proceeded at their own risk.

A few minutes following the mutineers departure, sounds of disaster reached Crowley's tent. Charles Adolphe Reymond had remained with him and, as he was still wearing his boots, elected to go out and offer what help he could. Again Crowley issued a warning that any attempt to descend at this point was risking unnecessary danger, but agreed to render help if Reymond returned with news that assistance was even a possibility.

Reymond did not return and no word was forthcoming. Crowley remained where he was for the night. in the morning, he made his descent and learned that Pache and three porters had fallen to their deaths, creating an avalanche which carried Righi and Guillarmod down the mountain and causing some injury.

In the lower camps Guillarmod admitted the foolishness of ignoring the advice of their climbing expert and bemoaned having to face Pache's family in Switzerland. Crowley departed for Darjeeling and withdrew the expedition funds from the bank, who had received telegraphed instructions not to surrender funds to the Englishman. According to Crowley's report the manager assumed Guillarmod had gone mad and was more concerned that the porters should be properly paid; a debt which was immediately honoured.

Guillarmod and Righi attacked Crowley in the Press and even cast blame on the porters. Crowley issued his own riposte, defending the natives, and promptly departed to lose himself in India where he could forget the disaster: sacrificing a goat in an ancient temple and hobnobbing with the Maharajah of Moharbhan near Calcutta.

The adventurer was starting to experience the onset of a dilemma. His wife Rose and their daughter were sailing to meet him in Calcutta and yet his heart yearned to liaise with his old lover Elaine Simpson, now in Shanghai. Visiting Allan Bennett in Burma was also on the magicians agenda.

Travelling on foot in the back alleys Calcutta to reach Culinga Bazar, a venue of promising sexual iniquity, Crowley shot two men with a revolver. He reports the event as a spur of the moment defense against mortal danger as he found himself in darkness, surrounded by men attempting to pin his arms to his side as an attempt to stab him at close quarters and then rob him.

Crowley collected Rose and his daughter Lilith from the dockside and told her, "You've arrived just in time to see me hanged." On the advice of his close friend Edward Thornton and a Calcutta lawyer they departed the subcontinent within days on an outgoing ocean liner bound for Rangoon.

4 Master of the Temple

Disembarking in Rangoon following an idyllic cruise through the silken waters of Burma's west coast, Crowley booked his family into a hotel and went to stay with Allan Bennett whom he found to be in a shocking state, both physically and mentally. Having moved beyond the novitiate grades of Buddhism, the disciplines of priesthood were taking their toll on Bennett. Crowley noted a general lack of hygiene and nutrition and was disappointed to find that Allan was pessimistic concerning the quest for the attainment of the state of enlightenment known as Samadhi. This, he recounted to his visitor, was a state which could only be achieved in harmony with sympathetic personal karma. It was, he explained, akin to finding oneself on the point of a wheel and expecting to touch a certain stone on the road; which would require a phenomenal amount of advance planning and strategy to place oneself correctly. This, he was beginning to believe, required more than intentionality and aspiration on the part of the individual.

Bennett was beginning to shift into an oriental mindset quite alien to the cultures of the industrialized West. One of the foremost ideas presented as teaching by the current Dalai Lama is how the contemporary western ego-mind expects everything to be explained to it, comparing this with the inquisitive innocence of a child. Some questions cannot be answered within a limited and immature frame reference. This is as true for the subtleties of mathematics as it is for matters of philosophy or religion. Allan Bennett's current state of grace, unenviable in terms of lack of material comforts and essential basic hygiene, had granted him certain depths of insight which were evidently lacking in his prior engagements with western Hermeticists.

Crowley too was beginning to show signs of maturity. Recently in India, his friend Edward Thornton had remarked upon the fragmented nature of Crowley's genius, echoing Eckenstein's earlier critique and planting a measure of self-doubt in his mind. His trials on mountain peaks and global travel experience had widened his cultural horizons. Men had died and the adventurer had experienced bitter failure in his sporting ambitions. His reputation as a gentleman had been brought into question in the Press. Crowley progressively turned his attention inwards from this point on and began to view his spiritual expectations in more refined terms than pure self-glorification.

Prior to this, Crowley had been operating on enthusiasm alone and concentrating only upon material results. On numerous occasions he had found magic too easy and abandoned the path after reporting allegedly spectacular results. In a manner typical of immature western modernity the universe had to bend down to him and explain itself. When he had explored the first two Enochian Aethyrs in Mexico, he reports titanic Angelic powers which noticed his presence. On an earlier visit to Egypt he had failed to revisit the Pyramids, noting in his diary that "I wasn't going to have forty centuries look down on me. Confound their impudence!"

All of a sudden, with the disappointment of Kanchenjunga behind him and his fortune beginning to dwindle the shadow of maturity was starting to fall over Crowley.

In terms of the Hermetic Qabalah as channeled by the Golden Dawn order, he had passed through the lower grades which are concerned with the purification of discrete elements of the Nephesh, or animal soul, and was now beginning to achieve an existential awareness emanating from the Ruach which Crowley describes as "the machine of the mind converging on a central consciousness."

Three days of Allan's pessimism was as much a dose of reality as Crowley could stand and he decided to take Rose and his baby daughter on an expedition to travel across the borders of South West China in an adventure to rival the exploits of his hero Richard Burton. Setting off from Mandalay, which he describes as a diseased swamp they proceeded by steamboat up the Irrywaddy and reached the borderlands of Indo China.

The British consul at Tengyueh, wrote, "I will say frankly that I had no idea that Mrs. Crowley or a child would be with you, and that while there is really no reason why they should not go to Yunnanfu, along the main road, they will, I fear, suffer a good deal of discomfort and inconvenience on the road from the inquisitiveness and impertinence of the Chinamen: which will try your temper. I would also recommend you to dress in Chinese style, and if Mrs. Crowley would not object to a Chinese lady's upper garment or jacket, she would attract much less attention and be less subject to annoyance."

Crowley was astonished at the idea that the natives could possibly fail to see him as an equal due to his natural nobility of purpose and everyman sense of fair-play. Nevertheless, he experienced a few minor travel impediments with local officials which were no doubt due to his refusal to be blackmailed through the demands for Baksheesh. Having been in receipt of a supportive telegram from Litton, he threatened retribution from his friend on high to secure the release of their passports after finding his progress delayed in Bamo.

Litton was everything Crowley could have wished for in terms of a Burtonesque British Consul manning an outpost at the edges of the world's greatest Empire. The adventurer describes him as governing the province through "the sheer strength of the superiority conferred by sympathy, integrity and moral courage."

Inviting the Crowleys to take advantage of the hospitality of the British Consulate, Litton also provided them with travel plans and accurate maps.   During their stay they learned of the death of seventeen people in riots raging in Shanghai and were exposed to local paranoia concerning an anti-foreign rising.   European colonial interference - particularly that of the French - was deeply unpopular.

Disaster was not long coming.   Litton, the English Consul, died suddenly in mysterious circumstances.   Crowley and fellow guest George Forrest believed him to have been poisoned. The only other possibility was that of a mystery jungle virus.   Both options were equally worrying.

Crowley kept his wife in isolation from any possible infection and purchased the remainder of Litton's canned goods from his Chinese widow; proceeding to Yunchangfu where he and Rose were entertained by the Mandarin with a twelve hour orgy of Chinese cuisine.

The following four months, when Crowley 'walked' across southern China have been the basis of much speculation. Some commentators have noted that the route which was selected would have been of great interest to the British Foreign Office. In later years, such as his time as resident of Berlin during the turbulent early 1930s, Crowley would forward reports of his observations of British nationals present in Berlin to Scotland Yard, Special Branch as a matter of course. One ex-Special Branch officer later complained to Everard Feilding, the Beast's intelligence contact in Whitehall, that the English magician was sending him intelligence reports which he was no longer cleared to read due to his retirement from the service.

During this period Crowley commenced a cycle of magical work which was purely internal; dependent upon the powers of visualization and concentration which Eckenstein had encouraged him to develop. On a daily basis, the magician would retreat into an all consuming trance as he rode across the southern Chinese provinces. These spiritual exercises consisted of the visualization of a complete set of Golden Dawn temple layouts, with appropriate symbolic furnishings, in which he engaged in a series of rituals and mental ceremonial performances designed to put him in touch with his Holy

Guardian Angel. At one point during his travels Crowley became so deeply immersed in these experiences he and his mule fell down a forty foot ravine. Fortunately, only his pride was wounded.

In his magical diaries of the period, and in those for years after, Crowley referred to these exercises using the Greek term Augoeides, which translates as 'shining' or 'celestial' body and refers to the Higher Astral Soul of the individual.

At the back of his mind, the delay over commencing the Abramelin operation which he had intended to start over two years earlier in Boleskine was beginning to irritate him. Early during April 1906 he had made a note to commence this operation properly on the Easter Sunday following. Later, writing in his autobiographical *Confessions*, Crowley reports that he was also experiencing dissatisfaction with the psychological aftermath of his experiences in Cairo 1904 and the reception of the *Book of the Law*.

Unlike many who enter into a study of the theory and practice of western magic, Crowley was a man of science and a skeptic. This is partly why he found his achievements in magic, particularly the visionary successes, so troublesome. After almost every major new milestone in his magical development, Crowley's instinctive reaction is to retreat from the field and go and play golf ... or climb a mountain.

Perhaps it was his deep childhood grounding in the lore of Old Testament religion combined with his vivid poetic imagination which made him a dab hand at Golden Dawn Qabalah. But his Cambridge science studies had instilled an observational discipline which revealed itself in his journals. Crowley's observations are deeply self-analytical. He would use a stop watch to record the duration of his exercises in visualization and make exact diary entries for later comparison. Two years later, writing in a journal which was published as *John St John*, he combined these exercises with a daily observance of noting every single act performed in the course of his daily duties as being performed for the glory of Adonai. This term technically translates from the Hebrew as *Lord*, being the substitution of choice for Jews choosing to avoid pronouncing the name Yehovah. In Crowley's system of metaphors,

Steven Ashe

Adonai represents the Holy Guardian Angel entity which informs the fabric of the spiritual identity on the higher planes lying above the realms of the Ruach and the Nephesh - the Soul and the Animal Intelligence.

The rational part of his mind was rejecting the whole subjective validity of the Book of the Law. He describes himself as being in revolt against it. The text of this curious piece of automatic writing is, in some places, highly personal to Crowley, addressing him as The Beast; the pet name given to him by his hysterically religious mother. At others, the work refers to changes in the ceremonial hierarchy of the celestial gods; hinting at the fall of Osiris and the rise of the youthful Horus. Much is made of Crowley's messianic role in the unfolding of a new age in mankind's spiritual development and there are whole passages of sublime prose poetry promising a glorious destiny for all who follow the way of the new aeon:

"Behold! these be grave mysteries; for there are also of my friends who be hermits. Now think not to find them in the forest or on the mountain; but in beds of purple, caressed by magnificent beasts of women with large limbs,

and fire and light in their eyes, and masses of flaming hair about them; there shall ye find them. Ye shall see them at rule, at victorious armies, at all the joy; and there shall be in them a joy a million times greater than this. Beware lest any force another, King against King! Love one another with burning hearts ....." (Book of the Law, Chapter One, Verse 61)

"But to love me is better than all things: if under the night stars in the desert thou presently burnest mine incense before me, invoking me with a pure heart, and the Serpent flame therein, thou shalt come a little to lie in my bosom. For one kiss wilt thou then be willing to give all; but whoso gives one particle of dust shall lose all in that hour. Ye shall gather goods and store of women and spices; ye shall wear rich jewels; ye shall exceed the nations of the earth in splendour & pride; but always in the love of me, and so shall ye come to my joy." (Book of the Law, Chapter Two, Verse 24)

For the previous seven years Crowley had immersed himself daily in the Golden Dawn system, through meditation, ritual and intellectual study. In a sense he had willingly brainwashed himself so that, on the deepest instinctive level, he continually interpret his personal destiny in terms of mythic archetypes. In as much as the rational part of his mind rejected the Book of the Law's call to spiritual greatness, another part of him yearned for confirmation that the whole Cairo experience could be validated in terms of the path of his Golden Dawn initiations.

One way or another he intended to find out. Only two people could be relied upon to give him the feedback he needed; George Cecil Jones back in England, or Elaine Simpson, his old girlfriend in the GD, now domiciled in Shanghai. Feeling an irresistible urge to cheat on his wife, Crowley chose the latter option and dispatched Rose and the baby, back to Calcutta to collect their luggage and sail with it back to England. Crowley proceeded directly to Shanghai.

Unfortunately for Rose, no doubt in low spirits at this sudden turn of events, the journey home was marked by the tragedy of the death of their daughter. According to Crowley's autobiography, the nurse which the couple had taken on to assist with the baby had taken flight early in their Chinese excursion and Rose had coped throughout without complaint. She had furthermore achieved an athletic physique through the trials of the journey and all reports point to her glowing health and high morale. In the heat of the India Ocean upon the return voyage, the baby's bottle teat had become infected and the child died of dysentery.

In the meantime, Crowley was unsuccessfully wooing Elaine Simpson in Shanghai. She still had her Golden dawn robes and agreed to practice ritual magic with him. He was disturbed to learn that Elaine had worn her robes and won first prize as a Wizard at a Fancy Dress party in Hong Kong, but she was fascinated by his tale of Aiwass and the whole idea of the Book of the Law.

Crowley writes: "The first result of my work with Soror F. was that immediately I told her of the work in Cairo, she said boldly and finally that she believed in the genuineness of the communication. I was infuriated. I believe my main object in going to see her had been to get encouragement in my revolt."

They began a series of rituals to encourage the spiritual manifestation of Aiwass, the entity who allegedly delivered the *Book of the Law* in Cairo. Elaine Simpson took on the role of seer and, after some general Golden Dawn rituals of banishing and consecration, Aiwass made himself visible to her in her astral vision whilst Crowley directed the line of questioning.

During the ritual, Simpson reported that Ra Hoor Khuit was sending blinding flashes of light and recounted Aiwass' instructions that Crowley should return to live in Egypt along with reassurances that money difficulties would be solved more easily than he feared. From his later accounts of this mediumistic enterprise it is evident that he was far from impressed. At the close of the ritual Crowley took advantage of the opportunity to seduce his magical partner, though the event was not sustained due to a certain feeling of mutual awkwardness.

Days after leaving Shanghai, he experienced a vision of a man being nailed to a cruciform table. Mysterious Adepts floated around him and he was informed by his astral guide that these were brothers of the mystical Order which he had been seeking:

*"Then, one, human, white, self-shining (my idea after all!) came forth and put his hands over mine, saying: 'I receive thee into the Order of ---
.'*

"I came back to earth in a cradle of flame. I was thus formally received among the Secret Chiefs of the Third Order on the astral plane."

The magician sailed back to Liverpool, via New York, feeling dejected about how things had turned out with Elaine Simpson. On another level he had experienced a catharsis in his attitude to the *Book of the Law*, experiencing a return to magical self-confidence. A fellow Golden Dawn adept had taken the work seriously and this gave him encouragement.

Stepping back onto British soil on June 2nd 1906, Crowley learned of the death of his daughter and experienced something of a mental and physical breakdown. After spending a few weeks recuperating in a nursing home on the south coast, during which time he mapped out the text of Liber 777 - a book of magical correspondences, he went to stay with George Cecil Jones to report on his magical workings in Shanghai. Jones put him through a higher grade Golden Dawn ritual and on 29th July they laid plans for a new occult order known as the A.'. A.'. (or Argentium Astrum) which was to be founded just over a year later.

During this period, Jones also encouraged

Crowley to take the oath of the Master of the Temple grade and join the Third Order. Since Crowley's split with Mather's, Jones had continued his English Golden Dawn associations under London lodge chief Florence Farr and was now claiming the grade of Adeptus Exemptus $7 = 4$. To all practical purposes the English Golden Dawn was no longer operational as a coherent body, having split over the issues of Mather's overbearing autocratic rule and also the consequences of the Horos scandal. Jones considered that he and his magical friend could do better.

During the following months, for a period of two years, Aleister Crowley penned a series of delightful and perplexing works of inspiration, similar in theme to the Book of the Law. These are collectively known as The Holy Books of Thelema.

In many respects these are works of cryptographic genius and, though filled with the same 'stream of consciousness' poetic symbolism of the Book of the Law are presented in intentionally cryptic formats.

Liber Ararita, a book of seven chapters each containing fourteen verses, is designed to be rearranged into fourteen chapters with seven verses each. According to notes made by Crowley later in life, one reads the first line of each chapter to arrive at the reconstructed chapter one. The second line of every chapter then becomes a reconstructed chapter two, and so on. Also, the numbers given in the book seem designed to be interpreted using an alternate number base system.

"Even for five hundred and eleven times nightly for one and forty days did I cry aloud unto the lord the affirmation of His Unity."

Five hundred and eleven in decimal becomes 777 when using Base 8 mathematics - and Forty one in decimal becomes 56 in Base 7.

Everything about *Liber Ararita* smacks of cryptography. The rearrangement of seven verses into fourteen, renders the sevenfold schemata of Creation both by day and by night. The work is a litany of the history of divine Creation and of mystical initiation. The word *Ararita* is associated with the Golden Dawn ritual of the hexagram, a symbol representing the balance of the planets know to the ancients around a solar centre. Whereas this sevenfold schemata has been taken to flights of fancy in early 20th century pseudopigraphia such as *The Kybalion*, the rudimentary knowledge of a genuine and ancient system of sevenfold classification known as The Seven Palaces was hinted at in Golden Dawn knowledge papers.

When the Hebrew letters are harmoniously distributed upon each of the seven palaces (and in the paths between) the arrangement conforms to calendric mathematics. The outer edges add up to 364, the length of the Hebrew year and certain words both in Hebrew stand out. Crowley employs these throughout the text. These are illustrated in Alrah Fraser's Aleister Crowley's Secret Temple and on Youtube within a video under the title *Liber Ararita*.

Another example of these inspired Holy Books is *Liber Colis - The Book of the Heart Girt with Serpent* which is resplendent in imagery consonant with the grandeur of the Book of the Law.

"Ah! my Lord Adonai, that dalliest with the Magister in the Treasure-House of Pearls, let me listen to the echo of your kisses.

"Is not the starry heaven shaken as a leaf at the tremulous rapture of your love? Am not I the flying spark of light whirled away by the great

wind of your perfection?

"Yea, cried the Holy One, and from Thy spark will I the Lord kindle a great light; I will burn through the great city in the old and desolate land; I will cleanse it from its great impurity."

Between October and December 1907 Crowley received a variety of literary works by methods of 'inspired' automatic writing. This collection of 'holy' books lie at the heart of Crowley's esoteric system known as *Thelema*. Even amongst its enthusiasts Thelema is mistaken for a new religion and this core collection of what Crowley later categorized as Class A Texts are pored over by contemporary students for their hidden mysteries.

Reunited with Rose and finding himself looking at the dwindling end of his fortune, he took a job as personal assistant to Lord Tankerville who was interested in Crowley's poetry. Tankerville suffered from what can best be described as a Bi-Polar condition whose excessive manias were exacerbated by a monumental cocaine habit. In addition to undertaking the smooth running of Lord Tankerville's affairs, Crowley would teach him magic and keep him from harm. Rose became an unofficial clairvoyant 'By Appointement' to His Lordship and somehow the couple survived several months with Tankerville, including an extended trip to Morocco, managing to keep a calm exterior whilst His Lordship was accusing all around him of involvement in a conspiracy to murder him.

Crowley was, by this time dallying with the responsibilities of the esoteric grade known as Master of the Temple whose corresponding oath includes the direction to interpret every event of existence as a particular dealing of God with one's soul. He took the oath of the Master of the Temple in the presence of Rose and Tankerville as witnesses. It would be two years before he fully claimed the grade, but he refers to himself several times in his correspondence and diaries of the era as a 'Babe of the Abyss'.

At the close of 1907 Crowley made the aquiantance of Captain JFC Fuller who had written a volume length critique of Crowley's philosophical genius in response to a competition in which the author offered a prize of £100. As the sole entrant, Fuller won the prize and accepted Crowley's offer to use the prize money to publish a lavish edition for general circulation. He became one of

Crowley's most influential pupils, later gaining fame as the most decorated soldier in the British Army, an early expert in Tank warfare and one of only two British guests at Hitler's fiftieth birthday party. He later became a member of Oswald Moseley's Fascist Black-Shirts.

Like Crowley, Fuller considered Christianity "historically false, morally infamous, politically contemptible and socially pestilential." In the pages of The Star in the West he professed himself an advocate of Crowleyanity. The hero worship was consummate and Crowley took to Fuller immediately.

It was Fuller who introduced another noteworthy disciple to his master, the poet Victor Neuberg - later Poetry Editor of the London Sunday Referee newspaper. According to his biographer Jean Overton-Fuller, Neuberg was the man who talent-spotted Dylan Thomas' and paid his train fare to London.

Crowley took to the younger Neuberg and recognized the capacity for magic within him. He took Neuberg under his wing and invited him to Scotland where the two men engaged in sado-masochistic homosexual encounters; the older Crowley whipping a naked Neuberg with stinging nettles and leaving him to suffer in a damp winter air with no bedclothes. The younger man's magical diary of the period records several experiences of astral projection where his astral body assumes the form of colourful geometric symbols.

Meanwhile Rose was drinking her way into oblivion; her husband discovered that she had ordered over one hundred and fifty bottles of whisky during his six months of absence from the country.

Jones and Crowley formally founded the magical order known as the A.'. A.'. in November 1907. In July of the the preceding year, when the two men had originally mooted the idea of their own magical order, Crowley noted in his diary that Jones wanted seniority. The latter had not yet laid eyes upon the Book of the Law and so far Crowley had only furnished access to his paraphrases of the translation of the text on the Stele.

In early 1908 he published the final version of his Collected Works, minus the Appendix containing the Book of the Law. He did send the proofs of this intended appendices to Captain Fuller, who retained it in his collection from whence it surfaced some decades later to see the light of day.

Fuller had reacted well. Even when informed that the work was a piece of automatic writing delivered by the hand of a mysterious Egyptian Adept named Big Beast, Fuller sang the praises of the work as displaying the hand of a true Master. The year previously Crowley had published *Konx Om Pax*, which includes the fabulous Wake World. Now he began to collaborate with Fuller on a complete overview of his magical diaries which were later published as *The Temple of Solomon the King*.

This piece was to form part of a projected series of volumes bound in hardcase to be published every six months in March and September entitled *The Equinox*. The journal was to be the mouthpiece of Crowley and Jones' new magical order the Argentium Astrum. The first edition was published on the spring Equinox, March 20th 1909. Alongside supplementary poetry and even comedy, The Equinox featured papers from the magical syllabus of the A.'.A.'. evolved from the traditional curriculum of the Golden Dawn. When Mathers learned of this he was furious and soon after launched a lawsuit to prevent further publication.

Frank Harris, London newspaper editor and owner of Vanity Fair magazine, contributed a piece entitled The Magic Glasses to The Equinox and reviewed the journal favourably in his publications. His association with the magazine owner brought Crowley to the attention of Harris' publishing rivals. Horatio Bottomley, publisher of John Bull, began to have him investigated by his journalists and then circulated a scurrilous leaflet accusing him of lining Cambridge undergraduates up for sodomy within the college dormitories. The Dean of Trinity College, Cambridge also accused Crowley of fishing for diciples amongst his students. Victor Neuberg and Norman Mudd were reprimanded and Mudd forced to abandon all association with the Master. Crowley had been invited to give a talk to a university society calling itself the Free-Thought Association and evangelical Christian opposition from within the faculty had stirred up a great deal of paranoia.

On June 28th, whilst searching for the paintings of the Golden Dawn Enochian Tablets in the attic, Crowley reports that he rediscovered the lost manuscript of the Book of the Law. The author Richard Cole asserts that all but page one of the manuscript is inscribed upon stock paper watermarked 1905. The cover sheet bears a 1904 watermark and was manufactured by the Gillie company based in Scotland. The remainder of the document is written on paper produced in London dated the following year. By this time, Crowley was either experiencing elements of false memory syndrome concerning the genesis of the Book of the Law or had fallen victim to a belief in his own propaganda. He had certainly evolved the reception myth to the point where Liber Legis was now presented as a messianic new age bible rather than as 'an example of automatic writing par excellence'.

Crowley introduced George Cecil Jones to the text of the Book of the Law, inducing him to acknowledge it as evidence of a communication from the hidden masters of the Great White Brotherhood. This assured Crowley of his superiority within the A.'. A.'. and he was now confident that he had superceded his original master in spiritual authority.

In the late summer, Crowley took Neuberg to London to assist with the production of forthcoming editions of *The Equinox.*

Unfortunately, despite selecting the finest leathers for binding, the choice of handmade paper and the quality of glue and stitching were insufficient to prevent the first editions from ageing gracefully. Few are known to survive in mint condition. Shortly after the magician had departed for his new London address, Rose left him and filed for divorce, claiming he had beaten her. Rose won custody of their daughter Lola Zaza.

Victor Neuberg was the first candidate to apply for admission to the outer grade of Probationer in the magical order of the A.'. A.'. He was in good company for that season's intake also included Kenneth Ward, Charles Stansfield Jones (Frater Achad) and the artist Austin Osman Spare who contributed artwork to two editions of *The Equinox*.

A year before Crowley had received his ticket to the Reading Room of the British Library and spent many fruitful days poring over the Enochian texts of Dr John Dee, court astrologer to Queen Elizabeth the First. Sixty years later the English occultist Robert Turner,, author of *The Heptarchia Mystica of John Dee*, reviewed these documents and found the handwritten scrawl of both Crowley and Mathers in Dee's margins. He observed that neither of these past masters had noticed that the original diagrams inscribed by Dee were mistakenly printed in reverse negative in early and all subsequent posthumous editions of Dee's writings. So much for their powers of studious observation.

The Enochian Tablets are complex squares of letters written in a strange logo-graphic font which have English alphabetic equivalents. These formed the ultimate talisman of Mathers' Golden Dawn synthesis of Planetary, Zodiacal and Hermetic symbolism.

At the close of 1909, Crowley and Neuberg travelled to Algiers and spent a month exploring the visions of the majority of Enochian Aethyrs which Crowley had turned aside from in Mexico. Employing the Enochian calls allegedly revealed to Dr John Dee and Edward Kelley in 1583, Crowley and Neuberg assumed the roles of the Elizabethan mage and his visionary Edward Kelley . The results are recorded in Liber 418, *The Vision and the Voice*, which represents Crowley's literary peak as a magical visionary.

Crowley shaved Victor's head, leaving only two tufts of hair which he twisted into horns and led him about the desert on a chain.

The two magicians walked across the sands of the Sahara desert, throwing themselves down in supplication to God and chanting verses from the Qur'an. Each dimension of the Enochian Tablets was explored, yielding highly symbolic visionary experiences. John Dee's original clairvoyant seer Edward Kelly was often suspicious, even occasionally contemptuous of the visions which he experienced. There was no real attempt on the part of Crowley and Neuberg to make much sense of the visionary content during the course of the recorded events. The whole scenario was far too psychologically immersive. As the magician stared into a topaz shew-stone set within a wooden crucifix the landscapes of the Angelic realm revealed themselves to him.

The visions as recorded by Neuberg, whom Crowley had appointed Scribe, were excursions into Golden Dawn Qabalistic symbolism peppered with archetypes from his own Book of the Law mythos:

"Whoso hath power to break open this sapphire stone shall find therein four elephants having tusks of mother-of-pearl, and upon whose backs

are castles, those castles which ye call the watch-towers of the Universe."

Other passages show the depth of visual detail which were summoned up in the mind's eye during these desert rituals:

"Now it is clear what she has woven in her dance; it is the Crimson Rose of 49 Petals, and the Pillars are the Cross with which it is conjoined. And between the pillars shoot out rays of pure green fire; and now all the pillars are golden. She ceases to dance, and dwindles, gathering herself into the centre of the Rose. Now it is seen that the Rose is a vast ampitheatre, with seven tiers, each tier divided into seven partitions. And they that sit in the Amphitheatre are the seven grades of the Order of the Rosy Cross. This Amphitheatre is built of rose-coloured marble, and of its size I can say only that the sun might be used as a ball to be thrown by the players in the arena. But in the arena there is a little altar of emerald, and its top has the heads of the Four Beasts, in turquoise and rock-crystal."

Crowley considered himself to have crossed the Abyss several times during this whole process, although he achieved the main success during his two attempts to access the 14th Aethyr. To prepare for this, he buggered Victor Neuberg on a hilltop for an aperitif.

The Crossing of the Abyss is a metaphor for the experience of gaining the initiation of the exalted grade Master of the Temple in Crowley's new improved Golden Dawn order the Argentium Astrum. In reality this whole dynamic takes place over a period of time. The visionary angelic light-show with its parade of meaningful symbols which were part and parcel of Crowley's expectations are not essential to this process. However, the magician and his partner were faithful to the spirit of the original Dee and Kelley workings in both visionary breadth and rhetoric. The cosmic scale of the visions which they experienced are on par with those in the ancient Book of Enoch.

The day previously, during the vision of the 15th Aethyr, Crowley had been examined by an assembly of initiates and recognized as a Master of the Temple. The vision of the 14th Aethyr sealed his initiation and he passed into the City of Pyramids and given the title Nemo - no man - having transcended the human part of himself.

"Presently my eyes beheld (what first seemed

shapes of rocks) the Masters, veiled in motionless majesty, shrouded in silence. Each one was exactly like the other. Then the Angel bade me understand whereto my aspiration led: all powers, all ecstasies, ended in this --- I understood. He then told me that now my name was Nemo, seated among the other silent shapes in the City of the Pyramids under the Night of Pan ..."

Only days later, during the vision of the 10th Aethyr, occurred one of the most well-known tales associated with Crowley and, as it turns out, this may simply never have happened. This was the occasion on which Crowley was possessed by the Demon Choronzon, who represents the dis-associative forces of the individual's subconscious mind which combine to prevent ultimate enlightenment. In the earliest extant Dee manuscripts the entities name is written as *Coronzom*.

According to Crowley's later reports, Neuberg was sitting within a protective magic circle drawn in the sand, whilst the demon of illusion was called to manifestation within a sacred triangle on the periphery. Whilst Neuberg was busy writing down a prolonged speech by

Choronzon, intended to distract him, the demon threw sand over the line of the protective circle thus breaking its perfect harmony. Choronzon then attacked the scribe in the form of a naked savage, at which Neuberg drove him back at the point of a dagger.

Victor Neuberg denied the account, claiming that he and Crowley had simply called forth the spirit of "a foreman builder from Ur of the Chaldees" according to Arthur Calder-Marshall. We shall never know the exact truth as, mysteriously; Crowley chose to tear out the pages where this encounter is described within the surviving manuscript of the events.

Delighted to have completed a cycle of work which confirmed his initiation into the grade of Master of the Temple in his own mind, he sank into a self-satisfied state of Samadhi.

The symbols detailed in *Liber 418 : The Vision and the Voice* form the basis of interpretations of Crowley's *Thelema* system and, for some, seem to have become the pillars of a new religion. This is not surprising, given the magician's deep familiarity with the lyrical metre of the King James Bible combined with his messianic expectations. Together with the

Book of the Law, Liber 418 stands as one of the two pillars of the magical house of Thelema. If, as Richard Cole suggests, Crowley created a copy of the manuscript on paper stock watermarked 1905 in order to 'work' the original material into a form more consistent with his evolving reception myth then the work is patently the product of human artifice. Similarly, the missing pages torn from Neuberg's handwritten account of the rituals in the Sahara may well signify the removal of inconvenient facts from the record. Crowley has admitted that, for reasons unfathomable even to himself, he deliberately forged incorrect diary entries around the period of the Cairo revelation in order to deliberately mislead. Could it be that he had forged an entire new religion and then taken refuge in false memory syndrome?

5 Through The Looking Glass

Crowley returned from Algeria having left George Rafflovitch, a disinherited heir to a vast fortune, in charge of the editorial office of The Equinox. Raflovitch was the son of a wealthy Odessa banker and a Countess descended from one of Napoleon's ministers of finance. After spending initial advances upon his inheritance, Rafflovitch's family had stepped in and restrained his wayward finances. Crowley had recognized a familiar spirit and taken the young man under his wing, introduced him to powerful friends and helped to arrange British citizenship. In his benefactor's absence the young emigré had written cheques and drawn upon bank funds by forging Crowley's signature whilst running up a number of unauthorized business debts. Rafflovitch was dismissed but more trouble lay on the horizon.

Golden Dawn chief MacGregor Mathers applied for a restraining order on a pending issue of The Equinox. He was incensed that the secrets of the higher grades of the Golden Dawn order were to appear in print in the third edition of Crowley's *Equinox*.

Although Mathers was successful throughout the original hearing held in Judge's chambers, Crowley soon had the decision overturned in court. The case came to the attention of the Fleet Street press and the Golden Dawn name was once again dragged through the mud. Ex Golden Dawn supremo Wynn Westcott wrote to FL Gardner noting the appearance of the case in the Broadsheets. Following this, Westcott managed to scotch Crowley's chances of entering English Freemasonry proper by putting the word out that the young man was not a wholesome prospect for membership. During 1911 and 1912 Crowley applied to a number of English lodges only to be met with a wall of silence.

After his successful rebuttal of Mathers' lawsuit, a tidal wave of psudo-masonic certifications flooded through the letterbox of the London offices of The Equinox. Crowley received a review copy of John Yarker's *The Ancient Schools* and entered into a correspondence with the author. Yarker was a man obsessed by Freemasonry who collected and invented ancient rites. He conferred upon Crowley the grades of 95° Memphis and 90° Mizraim.

Crowley writes: *"From this time on I lived in a perfect shower of diplomas, from Bucharest to Salt Lake City. I possess more exalted titles than I have ever been able to count. I am supposed to know more secret signs, tokens, passwords, grand-words, grips, and so on, than I could actually learn in a dozen lives. An elephant would break down under the insignia I am entitled to wear. "*

A continuous stream of casual visitors to his studio and offices insisted on their own credentials as leader of the Rosicrucian Order. One of the more plausible of these callers, Theodor Reuss, introduced himself as Grand Master of Germany of the combined Scottish, Memphis and Mizraim Rites of Freemasonry. Another set of titles accredited through Yarker. Reuss was a German Espionage agent circulating in England as a Music Hall entertainer whilst keeping an eye upon Karl Marx's daughter for the German government. He was also a guiding hand in the development of the late Karl Kelner's Ordo Templi Orientis, a pseudo Freemasonic organisation popularising the mysteries of sexuality in ritual. The Order was founded on lines similar to Max Theon's *Hermetic Brotherhood of Light* which is also another title the OTO used to describe itself.

In May Crowley, Neuberg and Leila Waddell performed an invocation of Bartzabel, the Spirit of Mars at the residence of fellow A.'. A.'. member Commander G.M. Marston. Now it was the turn of the poet Victor Neuberg to stand outside the magic circle in a magical triangle into which the spirit would be summoned.

Marston was interested in military intelligence concerning Germany and the great European powers. Neuberg, possessed by the spirit of Bartzabel, predicted an all encompassing European war within five years.

Crowley had conceived the idea of a series of semi public rites dedicated to the seven astrological planets, the Rites of Eleusis, and staged the ritual performances 'at home' at 124 Victoria Rd. Leila Waddell, his new Scarlet Woman, played violin at the performances and Victor Neuberg pranced around to the point of exhaustion in the style of a man in the grip of psychedelic drugs attempting the Riverdance. Crowley commented that it was the most astonishing spectacle of dance gymnastics. A mysterious potion rumoured to be exotic was passed around the audience whilst several ritual charades were enacted broken by moments of poetic oration or musical enchantment. The events were a success and Crowley rented Caxton Hall to repeat the rites for a public audience.

Because of the difference in venues, the rites which had worked so well in Crowley's studio were unsuited to the impersonal scale of Caxton

Hall which is the size of an average English country town hall. The coloured lamps and shadows cast by the robed temple officers possessed more dramatic impact in the intimacy of Crowley's studio.   In his Confessions he writes with regret that he did not spend as many weeks preparing for the event as he did minutes. He realized that his symbolism and insignia would get lost on so vast a stage and adopted the creative solution, holding the rites in complete darkness.   This, Crowley reasoned would heighten the instincts of the audience thereby creating a focus on the events upon the lamp lit stage.

Unfortunately *The Looking Glass*, a weekly sports newspaper specializing in scandal saw the dimly illuminated atmosphere as a breeding ground for active vice. Rumours spread that the audience was being offered a potion spiked with drugs. The Looking Glass ran a campaign against Crowley and dragged in the good name of his friends Allan Bennett and George Cecil Jones. The former was still in the Far East, the latter was a self-employed analytical chemist who regularly published in the academic press. Jones resented implications in *The Looking Glass* that his association with Crowley blackened his name and sued the newspaper for libel.

Crowley's reputation was being dragged over the coals in the gutter press and many of the insinuations were based on truth. He had been painting himself as the bad boy for so long that his reputation was beginning to catch up with him. Lawyers working for Jones took all precautions in keeping Crowley from the witness stand. Council acting as Defence for *The Looking Glass* quoted passages from some of Crowley's pornographic poetry. Dr Berridge of the Golden Dawn appeared as a witnesses and bore testament to the vagueness of Crowley's replies when Berridge had put it to him that there were rumours of immoralities at the young man's Chancery Lane apartments; he had neither confirmed or denied the matter.

Jones lost the case. Not at all surprising considering Crowley was a little too hot to handle for polite society. The bohemian atmosphere of his Fulham Road studio was more typical of a Notting Hill hippy squat some sixty years later. His Diary of July 1910 records a scene in which he and Leila Waddell, Victor Neuberg and Charles Stansfield Jones locked themselves in the front sitting room and burned heads of Indica Cannabis on a charcoal brazier, filling the atmosphere with a thick smog. A member of Hawkwind or the Grateful Dead could not have felt more at home.

Victor Neuberg had fallen in love with Jeanne Heyse, an actress performing under the name Ione de Forest who had been recruited to supplement the performance of Eleusis at Caxton Hall. Jeanne was a chronic depressive and lived on her nerves, often threatening suicide. Crowley was livid with jealousy and stalked her at home, walking up to her door and drawing a mystic Tau cross along with the symbol of Saturn in a dire curse. She later killed herself with a pistol. Neuberg never truly forgave Crowley for his part in this sordid affair.

The bad publicity arising from trial and the perception that Crowley should have stood alongside Jones to defend his reputation caused an exodus of pupils from the ranks of the Argentium Astrum. Even Crowley's devoted cheerleader Captain Fuller turned against his hero and threatened to withdraw from writing the latest installment of The Temple of Solomon the King unless certain demands were met.

Crowley was not to mention him by name in public or in private and should pay Fuller £100 for every breach of this directive. The magician was furious. Relations between the two thereafter were strained and distant. Gerald Yorke, later a pupil and financier of Crowley told a BBC interviewer that the final split between pupil and master came when Fuller opened his daily post at the Breakfast table only to find Crowley had sent him a collection of bawdy seaside postcards. This turned out to be a step too far for the stuffy military man.

Crowley and Neuberg returned to Algeria to escape the fallout. Hiring a motor car they explored the coast, but did no more magic. Crowley was still puffing out his chest at the notion that he had transcended his human ego, writing "I had no business to take part in the affairs of men by personal contact with them in their sheepfolds, monkey houses and pigstys." This was surely the most atypical case of Ego loss ever experienced.

Crowley divided much of his time during 1911 between London and Paris where he wrote the play *Adonis* and some of his best poetry. His *The Ghouls* was celebrated in The Poetry

Review as "the most ghastly death dance in English Literature."

In London, the magician arranged a series of public magical displays at his studio in Fulham to rival the reputation of the Rites of Eleusis and hopefully provide funds to supplement his diminishing fortune. One patron, the writer Elliott ODonnell later wrote about his experiences at one of Crowley's evening performances. He claimed that in the darkness Crowley read from a work called *The Book of Death* following which he was serenaded by a host of women playing harps whilst emerging from wooden boxes. American writer Harry Kemp reports Crowley sitting before a black altar decorated with a serpent and a gold circlet chanting "There is no Good. Evil is Good. All hail, Prince of the World to whom even God himself has given dominion."

In October, 1911 a chance meeting in Hyde Park with Isadora Duncan, the famous dancer, and her best friend and assistant Mary D'Sturges led to Crowley making his mark. Dressed in a bright and gaudy Hawaiian shirt and matching knickerbockers, and high on drugs, Crowley displayed eye teeth which had been filed to a point and kissed the ladies hands, drawing blood. Days later he attended a party celebrating Mary's birthday. After a brief courtship Crowley travelled with her to Switzerland.

Arriving in Zurich, Crowley plied his new sexual partner with vast quantities of alcohol. Eventually she started to spout spiritual gibberish, claiming to have a message for him from an invisible individual. After listening with some cynicism for over an hour, the magician began to notice that certain statements she made could only be explained through either psychic means or through an intimate familiarity with his personal history.

Travelling onto St Moritz, one of the magician's favourite continental hang-outs, the pair booked into the Palace Hotel and began a series of rites in which Crowley encouraged a combination of the effects of sexual exhaustion and narcotics to induce visions in the mind's eye of his partner. Over the next eleven days, in four separate workings, Mary provided a series of messages from a discarnate intelligence which included Qabalistic number ciphers and messages concerning a mysterious *Book Four* which Crowley was commanded to write.

Steven Ashe

Crowley had a vision himself; an image of a property surrounded by Persian Nut trees. Moving on to Rome the couple came across a villa for rent where such trees were in evidence in the courtyard. They rented it immediately and set to work with Mary manning the typewriter to create the classic work on entry level Yoga which would eventually become included as the first section of Crowley's magnum opus *Magick in Theory and Practice*. In addition to this, they prepared embryonic structures for what would later be included in part two of this work as a study of the theories of esoteric magic.

Mary's teenage son Preston finished the school term and joined the couple at the villa. Crowley describes the lad as "a most god-forsaken lout". Preston was later to become one of Hollywoods most respected film directors during the 1930s. He found his mother preoccupied with her new lover and carried only distateful memories of the man who encouraged her into alcoholism and drug abuse. Perhaps it was Preston's influence which pulled the couple apart, for Mary soon became disenchanted with Crowley and he returned to Fontainbleu, France where his girlfriend Leila Waddell took up the reins and helped him knock part three of *Book Four* into shape.

Crowley maintained an open relationship with Australian violinist Leila Waddell and made her a central part of his magical practice. He also became her manager and guided her career and playing style with Svengali like attention. In 1912 he published the Book of Lies, featuring full page black and white portraits of his new Scarlet Woman in ritual poses. This work is a collection of ninety three chapters, the numerology of the word *Thelema*, which hover between the styles of Sufi mystery tales and Zen koans. Chapter twenty five deals with the Pentagram; Chapter seventy two is delineated *Shemhamphorash* referring to the 72 Angelic powers of the Qabalah. The work is of great interest to those wishing to gain familiarity with the puzzle of the mind of Aleister Crowley and his idiosyncratic development of the themes of Qabalistic magic.

In 1912 Theodore Reuss paid a visit to the magician's studio during which he stated that Crowley had laid bare the innermost secret of the Ordo Templi Orientis. Crowley was perplexed. He had no idea what Reuss was talking about he replied, at which Reuss opened a copy of *The Book of Lies* to the chapter titled The Star Sapphire and read from the contents: *"Let the adept be armed with his magic rood and provided with his mystic rose."* The penny dropped rood was code for the phallus and mystic rose for the vagina.

Crowley was inducted into the OTO grade of the Ninth Degree along with Leila Waddell in June 1912. The whole experience of rubbing along with Reuss and the continental initiates of the Order was to prove somewhat chequered. Crowley was promoted to the Grand Master of his own British wing of the Order, the Mysteria Mystica Maxima and given the title of 'King of Ireland'. As Grand Master he took the magical title *Baphomet* - supposedly the name of the idol worshipped by the Templars in the fourteenth century and illustrated by Eliphas Levi in the style of Typhon. The Egyptian god of darkness had crept into Tarot iconography to represent the Devil trump in two decks published during the sixteenth century which forever changed the way future artists would portray the figure of this card.

From this point on he was able to introduce a new dimension of magic into the pages of his journal The Equinox. The official organ of the rites and teachings of the A.' A.'. now became the spokespiece of the British OTO. Sexual magic became suddenly in vogue and Crowley found the benefits of his association with this particular magical fraternity were enriched by the one hundred pounds initiation fee he was able to charge. As he had spent the majority of his inheritance he wasted no time in issuing a prospectus displaying a flattering picture of Boleskine House, which he had signed over to the OTO in order to forestall his creditors, as an example of the material assets of his august fraternity. Now that his divorce from Rose was finalized, Crowley chose to start a trust fund which would pay dividends to Lola Zaza and himself in years to come. Rose was independently wealthy having inherited the estate of her first husband after his demise. In the meantime, there were no shortage of seekers willing to part with hard cash in return for recognition from the OTO in the form of certification.

Crowley took the mysteries of sexual magic seriously. Although he had some prior experience with introducing sexual elements into ritual practice, he had made no systematic study of the possibilities. Reuss introduced Crowley to the concept of employing the sexual fluids as sacramental elixirs and the OTO methods of sexual practice, both solo and for couples. Within a year, he had rewritten most of the OTO initiation rituals to incorporate symbolic elements of Thelema. In true Crowley style, references to the Beast and the Scarlet Woman, the Goddess Nuit and of course Ra Hoor Khuit would henceforth find their way into the OTO canon which, previous to Crowley's involvement, contained no such elements. This did not go down at all well with many of the German lodges of the OTO and it was not until after the death of Theodore Reuss in the 1920s that the whole organization would be brought under Crowley's full autocratic control.

Like many pseudo masonic organizations, outside of sex magic the Oriental Templars specialised in rites dedicated to admitting new members and advancing them through a series of grades with grand but meaningless ceremonial titles. These included Scotch Mason, Knight of Rose-Croix, Grand Master of Light and Illuminatus.

Vittoria Cremers, an Italian Baroness who had

been involved with the editorial of Lucifer the magazine of the Thesophical Society, was recruited to manage property owned by the British OTO. She later fell foul of Crowley, who accused her of swindling the Order funds, and in turn accused him of having fallen from grace due to his mono-maniacal preoccupation with sex. Despite Crowley's reputation as a sex maniac, his pupil Gerald Yorke assures us that his master's magical diaries written between this time and the date of his death never recorded more than a hundred and fifty six orgasms in any given year. Crowley was meticulous with his records of sexual encounters and this figure is taken to be authoritative.

In addition to the nine grades of OTO membership, Crowley introduced an eleventh degree to cater for sexual operations of a homosexual nature which appealed to his tastes.

It was during 1912 that Crowley finally published Liber 31, a facsimile of the manuscript of The Book of the Law in edition seven of his journal *The Equinox*. The following year saw him resident in Moscow as the tour manager for Leila Waddell's vaudeville group The Ragged Ragtime Girls. Crowley had helped his mistress put the band of travelling players together and helped to oversee a successful debut at the Tivoli in London. In Moscow he wrote some of his most powerful lyric poetry including the splendid *Hymn to Pan*.

The break in his relationship with George Cecil Jones seems to have removed any inhibitions the magician might have had about proclaiming his automatic writing in Cairo, 1904 as a direct voice communication from the gods themselves. This seems to be the point where Crowley made the transition from being an occultist to becoming a cultist. During the late 1970s when the present author came across the first reprints of *The Equinox* in hardback, there was much speculation that Crowley had in fact been thrown back from the Abyss during the working recorded in The Vision and the Voice. Some commentators even inclined towards the uncharitable view that he was really nowhere near the required state of spiritual development where he might legitimately attempt such an operation. Others have suggested the whole thing was a projection of a much earlier stage of initiation associated with the Dominus Liminus grade prior to achieving the status of Adept.

Crowley's Choronzon is a similar figure to the Dweller upon the Threshold, the shadow-self of Jungian symbolism, who must be confronted before the aspirant may truly call himself Adeptus Minor.

There is an expectation that any Adept performing such an ambitious venture as attempting to cross the Abyss should have transcended the juvenile complexes which haunt each of us as we evolve through the stages of physical maturity. Crowley's identification with the Beast of the Apocalypse, a nickname his mother had taunted him with, seems to have become magnified to a degree where it became an omnipresent obsession. Not too many people forge an apocalyptic religion from the details of their Honeymoon. On the other hand, it takes more than token acts of defiance to bring about a revolution. The wholehearted manner in which Crowley took upon himself the responsibility to overthrow the culture of hypocrisy which defined Victorian Christianity shows the desperation of a tortured soul driven to extremes.

Ambivalence is a quality typical to tortured souls and, true to form. Crowley's essay

Steven Ashe

Energized Enthusiasm published in the March 1913 edition of *The Equinox* celebrated the esoteric link between wine, women and song as the sex and drugs and rock & roll of the magical path. However, the close of this year would see Crowley engaging in a six week homosexual orgy of sex magic in Paris with Victor Neuberg and New York Times Foreign correspondent Walter Duranty.

This series of rites of sexual magic combined elements of Golden Dawn magical theory with the sexual teachings Crowley had picked up from Reuss and the OTO. Concentrating upon gaining the benign and wealth building influence of planetary Jupiter and the inspirational effect of Mercury, Crowley and Neuberg combined energies raised by the sexual act to attract these qualities of the heavenly powers. Walter Duranty provided a series of Latin versicles which the sex ritualists would chant when on the point of orgasm.

A curious phenomenon which Crowley noticed concerned the results of the rituals when a mistake had been made in the performance of the ceremony. In one instance where the god Mercury who is sacred to communication failed to be charmed by the sexual events of the ritual, all contact with the outside world mysteriously ceased. Crowley had ordered daily news reports from London which suddenly ceased to arrive, as did their mail. Following one of the invocations of Jupiter, Neuberg came into an inheritance and donated five hundred pounds for the use of the Order.

Jane Cheron, one of Crowley's mistresses, visited and witnessed Crowley being buggered by Walter Duranty. This was purportedly an attempt by the magician to escape all sense of shame over the fulfillment of what he considered to be his 'natural' instincts.

This was to be the last time that Neuberg and his master performed magic together. Victor's parents intervened, concerned that their son was being both corrupted and fleeced by an older man. They never saw one another again. Crowley was soon to depart for America where he would spend five years working for the war effort in his own inimitable way. According to Jean Overton Fuller writing in her biography of Neuberg, when Crowley did return, Victor was settled with a new wife and child in a bungalow on the south coast of England. The returning mage stood outside the property for some time shouting "I want Victor" but the door remained firmly shut. Neuberg's new wife had been forewarned.

Much has been made of Crowley's involvement in pro-German propaganda in New York during the First World War, when he worked as the Editor of The International - a German leaning weekly newspaper. Crowley used this journal as a vehicle for his own poetic talents, advertising for the OTO and to pen a series of 'over the top' journalistic pieces praising the Kaiser and all things German. William Joyce, Lord Haw Haw, was hanged for as much following his broadcasts on Berlin Radio during World War Two. Why this fate never befell Crowley has mystified many of his biographers. Recent research has uncovered the fact that the American authorities wanted to arrest Crowley, but were told that he was operating with the knowledge and consent of elements within the British government. This rings true. Crowley reports that soon after his arrival in New York he inspected a large petro-chemical plant and then toured the southern states to gauge the popular mood concerning the European war.

Crowley arrived in America on the *Lusitania* with only fifty British pounds worth of currency. In New York he persuaded a collector of rare books and manuscripts to part with nearly eight hundred dollars for editions of his occult works, although he was expecting considerably more. Fortunately the editor of the American printing of *Vanity Fair* took a liking to a piece which Crowley had submitted and gave him a series of commissions which helped to pay his rent.

In 1915 he was sitting on the top deck of a bus travelling down fifth avenue reading some English Press reports when he was tapped on the shoulder by an Irishman named O'Brien who asked him if he supported a fair deal for Germany and Austria. Crowley assented, not revealing that his thoughts were "how much nicer Germans and Austrians would be if they were cut up into little squares and made into soup." O'Brien gave him his card, excusing himself as he had to alight from the bus at the following stop, telling him that he would be delighted to continue the conversation at his office address.

When he did call, O'Brien was nowhere in evidence. Instead, Crowley found he had stumbled upon the offices of *The Fatherland*, a literary engine of pro-German propaganda and was introduced to George Viereck who appeared to be the mastermind of the operation. Viereck had founded another newspaper, *The International* with similar pro German leanings which Crowley would be invited to edit when The Fatherland went into receivership. In his *Confessions*, Crowley drops the name of a Captain Gaunt, the New York based British Intelligence contact with whom he maintained a correspondence concerning his affairs with the Germans. Unfortunately for Crowley, Gaunt denied that any official sanction for the magician's activities involving the Germans was extended to the self styled spy. Gaunt did pass on Crowley's offer to work surreptitiously for the British cause to his contacts at the Foreign office and after due consideration they forwarded notice of a test question which, if Crowley were to prove at all useful, he should be able to obtain the answer to. In his *Confessions* the budding Magus accuses British Intelligence of expecting their espionage agents to act as if they were investigative journalists rather than fulfilling his expectations of what a spy ought to be involved with. He refused the test and was thereafter treated as a loose cannon.

Continuing to insist that he was proceeding with the knowledge and collaboration of British Intelligence, Crowley reports that he was able to pass himself off as a disaffected pro-Sinn Fein supporter and wrote a series of creative articles for The International which could be interpreted in a number of ways. One of these employed a particular brand of English humour, celebrating the German Kaiser in outrageous terms which passed unrecognized beneath the nose of the German editors. Crowley sent a copy of this article to Paul Carus in England who edited *The Open Court* and was widely known to publish more or less anything. A London bookseller was sentenced to three months hard labour for selling the edition in which this article appeared. Crowley noted that the war had caused the English to lose their sense of humour. Another article succeeded in persuading the Germans that the passenger ship *Lusitania* was equipped as a man of war. When the ship was sunk with all hands on board, the world reacted in horror against Germany. He counted this as a personal triumph.

Having sent for Leila Waddell, his ongoing Scarlet Woman, Crowley staged a highly public political showcase in which he burned an envelope containing his British Passport and threw it into the sea at the foot of the Statue of Liberty, declaring himself a true son of Ireland. News of the event was published in the New York Times on July 13th 1915, lending some credibility to his claim to Sinn Fein sympathies, if only in his own imagination. It is barely realistic that any genuine political freedom fighter would have accepted his theatrical claims with any degree of seriousness.

Leaving New York for a visit to the West Coast, he stopped off in Detroit where he was given a tour of the Parke Davis chemical works In Chicago he failed to succeed in having his genius for verse recognized by Narnet Munroe, the editor of a journal entitled *Poetry*, and then headed north for Canada where he was entertained by Charles Stansfield Jones, Fuller's ex student in the A.'. A.'. who had emigrated to Vancouver prior to World War One.

Crowley was impressed with the efforts which Jones and his associates had made on behalf of the OTO in Canada. They had built a chapter house and received their master with enthusiasm. He was sad to leave after spending a few days being feted and entertained, heading for the U.S. west coast by train.

Stopping in San Francisco only long enough to assure himself that the city had been satisfactorily rebuilt, he moved quickly on to Santa Cruz and then Los Angeles which he describes as full of "cinema crowd of cocaine-crazed, sexual lunatics, and the swarming maggots of near-occultists."

Eventually finding himself in New Orleans Crowley reviewed the quality of prostitution services in the Spanish and French quarter, finding the perversions available superior to those elsewhere save the fleshpots of Cairo. His attempts to connect with Freemasons in the city went unrecognized, with at least one Mason denying recognition of his handshake and annoying Crowley enough for him to mention the event in his memoirs.

A visit to Florida, saw Crowley reunited with one of his cousins and he settled on the Bishop's farm for a number of weeks before returning to Manhattan. By now the magician was completely bereft of funds and returned to New York, grateful to squeeze twenty dollars in salary per week from a career as editor and contributor to *The International*, the sister paper of Viereck's pro-German *Fatherland*. To supplement his income he wrote for Vanity Fair, held drug parties and attempted to market a new card game called Pirate Bridge he had invented.

During 1916 Alice Ethel Coomaraswamy became pregnant with Crowley's child. Alice, an English born Musician and wife of Indian Art historian Ananda Coomaraswamy, chose to leave Crowley and return to her husband in England. Setting sail from New York, she miscarried during the voyage and the magician henceforth blamed her husband for the death of his unborn child.

Later that year, Crowley performed a series of sex-magick operations with Jeanne Robert Foster for the purpose of engendering a magical child. Foster was well known as a poetess and as the editor of *The American Review of Reviews*. She was also a close friend of Ezra Pound, the poet WB Yates and his father, the painter John Butler Yates. Though married, she fell in love with her magical English suitor and even considered divorcing her husband to marry him. Again, Crowley was disappointed and claimed five years later that Jeanne had broken his heart. By way of karmic compensation for his loss, he received a letter from Charles Stansfield Jones informing his master that he had spontaneously taken the oath of Master of the Temple. This was an unorthodox decision, as Jones was only a Neophyte of the A.'. A.'. at the time. However, in Crowley's system it is legitimate for any aspirant to take the oath of Master of the Temple whatever their esoteric grade of development. This news left Crowley free to assume the oath of Magus, having fulfilled the requirement to introduce a successor to take on the responsibilities of the Master of the Temple grade he was vacating. Crowley decided that Jones, Frater Achad, was his magical son.

In between bouts of sporadic work, Crowley underwent a series of magical retirements which saw him retreat into the wilderness with hardly a dollar in his pocket along the coastline north of Long Island. During one such excursion, Crowley assumed the grade of Magus after concluding a ritual performed in the wild in which a frog was anointed as the Messiah, crucified and then toasted for lunch. A peculiar ritual. Occasionally a random devotee, or Scarlet Woman of the hour would rendevous with him to bring him food and wine.

In late 1917, shortly after completing the text of

his novel *Moonchild,* Crowley began living with Doctor of Chemistry Roddie Minor in her New York apartment studio. Roddie Minor had been a leading light in the public New York suffragette movement and was living apart from her husband. She is described by Crowley as a sensual, matronly type . In a series of sex-magick workings Roddie was sexually mounted simultaneously by Crowley and his homosexual lover Walter Gray, a negro jazz musician, in an exhaustive variety of combinations. Hashish and opium were liberally administered to encourage spiritual visions - the idea being to exhaust the priestess to the point where continued orgasm became analogous to a mind-set consonant with near death experience; the hallmark of the psychological mechanism of ritual initiation.

Roddie Minor claimed to be a natural clairvoyant and took to her role with enthusiasm. On the evening of Sunday January 14th 1918, smoking opium whilst Crowley sat writing what would be later published as *Liber Aleph: he Book of Wisdom & Folly,* Roddie cast her mind into the dimensions of the astral plane and described what she saw. After half an hour of listening to what he describes as spiritual gibberish, Crowley was surprised to hear his

Scarlet Woman begin to speak of symbols which resonated with his prior mystical experiences. The vision was of an egg beneath a palm tree. Six years before, the entity known as Ab ul Diz had instructed the magician to seek such a symbol in the Great Desert.

Crowley was suddenly interested. Roddie began to speak of an astral figure she initially called the 'Wizard' who revealed himself later as the entity known as Amalantrah. The operations continued until early Spring and Crowley obtained several revelations which he considered notable. To test the veracity of the information given by his otherworldly source, he asked Roddie to obtain the true spelling of his magical name in the OTO - *Baphomet*. The spelling returned by the priestess included the addition of a final letter R. When Crowley added up the gemetria value of this new spelling he found it added to 729 the cube of 9. He also noted that the name Amalantrah similarly adds to 729.

During the several weeks of esoteric workings Roddie was sometimes sexually mounted simultaneously by Crowley and his homosexual lover Walter Gray, a negro jazz musician, in an exhaustive variety of combinations. In some episodes of this sex and drug reverie Roddie beheld strange entities with many limbs, experienced herself as thirteen women being caressed simultaneously and continued to mantain astral liaisons with the Wizard Amalantrah who placed his arm comfortingly around her and informed her "It's all in the egg."

Some contemporary adherents of Crowley's magick regard the Amalantrah workings as an operation which opened the world to 'trans-plutonian' extra-terrestrial influences. It was during this late New York period that Crowley painted his famous portrait of one of the higher masters known as Lam which resembles modern depictions of the Grey type of alien in some respects. What Aleister Crowley would have thought of this interpretation of his artistic work is anyone's guess.

Throughout 1918 Crowley continued to explore the Amalantrah thematics in a series of sexual workings using a variety of partners of either sex. The complete record of sexual workings engaged in during this period are to be found in his diary accounts published as *Rex de Art Regia.*

Crowley went through a succession of sex-magick partners at such a high rate that Leila Wadell, the previous love of his life, could not bear his continual infidelities and left in exasperation. Roddie Minor similarly fell foul of Crowley's penchant for playing the numbers game. A young school teacher, Leah Hirsig visited Crowley's studio with her sister Alma who was interested in Theosophical matters. Crowley met them both at the door and immediately started to kiss Leah before even formal introductions could be made. He asked her to model for one of his portraits. She asked him to paint her as a Dead Soul. By January 1919, Leah took the oath of the Scarlet Woman and remained his sex-magick partner for the next six years.

Crowley's period in America had left him with something of a bad taste in his mouth concerning the commercialism with which so called spiritual knowledge was being sold to the people. In his Confessions he complains: *"The most famous astrologer in the States, who makes fifty thousand dollars a year, did not know that the solar system was essentially a disk. She thought the planets were stuck at random in the sky like so many plums in a suet pudding."* He met countless claimants to the chieftainship of Rosicrucian guilds - none of whom had even heard of the famous historic Rosicrucian manifestos such as the *Fama Fraternitatis* or *The Chemical Wedding of Christian Rosencrantz.*

Crowley had little business left to conduct in the United States. The International, the newspaper which he had single handedly kept afloat through a series of articles upon Magick and tongue in cheek pro-German propaganda, had been sold out from beneath him. Viereck accepted an offer from a Professor Keasbey retired from the University of Austin, Texas who had no further use for Crowley's literary talent. The periodical went into receivership swiftly after the business changed hands which raises suspicions that it was closed deliberately and that Keasbey was an intelligence department straw-man. Crowley was not to see Viereck again for over ten years. His final contact with the German propaganda master was by letter in 1936 when Crowley wrote encouraging Viereck to put the 'religion' of Thelema at the disposal of tyrant Adolf Hitler and the Nazis. No reply was received.

6 The Abbey of Thelema & Beyond

Two years before leaving America, on May 14th 1917 Crowley's mother Emily died leaving him £3,000 (around $140,000 by contemporary values). On the same day Special Branch police officers raided the Jermyn Street offices of the MMM, the London branch of the OTO, claiming that its proprietor was a German spy and a known traitor to his country.

When news of the raid reached him the magician assumed that Everard Feilding had arranged the raid to lend support to his espionage 'cover'. Unfortunately, this was the real thing and OTO Treasurer G.M. Cowie was intimidated by aggressive police Inspectors, as he had been on several instances before this. The police cleared the Jermyn Street offices of furniture and paperwork and arrested Mary Davies who was practicing as a clairvoyant from the premises as well as officiating at semi-public OTO rituals in her capacity as a Fifth Degree officer of the order.

In his *Confessions* Crowley accuses his treasurer Cowie of going insane and selling Crowley's Scottish mansion along with his remaining possessions for a song. In this matter Cowie was ill served by his order superior for he had spent a goodly portion of his retirement funds maintaining the London office and keeping up payments on the mortgage on Boleskine. By the time the state had finished prosecuting Mary Davies in the courts and denied her appeal, the lady clairvoyant was over two hundred and fifty pounds out of pocket. Cowie, who along with Crowley had not really been impressed with Mary's Spiritualism, nevertheless appreciated her effectiveness in the maintenance of her official OTO duties. She had attached herself to the magician following the public performances of the Rites of Eleusis at Caxton Hall. Following this she had made herself indispensible to the administration of the OTO and was very popular, opening doors for the Order in social circles where Crowley might have been rebuffed.

Davies and Cowie sold Boleskine House for £2,500 along with Crowley's personal effects and sporting equipment. Deducting the personal monies due to them for supporting the financial running of the organization, the remaining funds were wired to Crowley in America. This gave him the wherewithal to leave the country and depart for Europe in 1919 where he was to launch his ultimate experiment in promoting Thelema as an alternate lifestyle.

Following a delightful few months on the southern edge of the Forest of Fontainebleau, where he was joined by Leah Hirsig, the pair performed divination by means of the *I Ching* which led them to believe a move to Sicily would be favourable.

Leah had been born in Switzerland and held a dual nationality passport with United States citizenship. She had been visiting her family in the alpine paradise whilst the Beast lingered long enough in London to arrange the payment of the inheritance bequeathed by his mother. He certainly needed the money for Leah was pregnant with his child.

On the voyage across the Atlantic, they had made the acquaintance of Ninette Fraux Shumway, a nursery governess travelling with her young son who needed a job. Crowley made her an offer and by January of 1920 they found themselves living together in Fontainebleau. Leah joined them in March having given birth to a baby girl, Anna Leah whom they nicknamed Poupee.

Initially, Sicily was a disappointment. The hotel was sordid, dirty and disgusting. Crowley, who had survived the most trying physical challenges during his world travels, resolved that he could not spend a single further night there. Luck was on his side. The next morning a man appeared who declared he had a villa to rent. They took the residency after Crowley found that it had the same Persian nut trees growing in the garden which had influenced his decision to rent a villa in Italy with Mary D'Sturges ten years earlier during the Abul ul Diz workings. Surely this was a sign from the gods.

This was the Villa Santa Barbara where Crowley was to found his Abbey of Thelema, a communal environment where residents would be free to find and pursue their True Will.

After installing Ninette in the property and fixing both the plumbing and plastering, they were soon after joined by Leah and baby Poupee and then by a succession of guests; most of whom were prepared to pay Crowley for the privilege of studying magick under his tutelage. One of the first of these was Janc Wolfe, a Hollywood character actress from the silent era movies and longtime admirer of The Beast's writings.

Jane arrived at the abbey full of stress and angst. Crowley found her abrasive and packed her off for three weeks isolation camped in a tent near the edge of a nearby cliff. Once per day a child would bring her bread and water and leave without speaking. This was an exercise based upon a realization that Crowley had been gifted with during his American magical retirements. After a sufficient period of solitude the automatic mechanisms which drive us will relax allowing the natural spirit within a chance to thrive. After a period of ten days, Jane began to experience a continual thrill of inner bliss. Crowley's methods brought back her natural strengths and she eventually moved back into the Abbey to become a vital member of the community.

Another early recruit to the community was C.F. Russell, who later founded the sex magick based Choronzon Club which operated out of Chicago in the 1930s. Russell had met Crowley at his New York apartment in 1918 and received an entry level grade within the OTO. Russell joined Crowley in Cefalu following a dishonorable release from the US Navy after injecting himself with 40 grains of Cocaine and nearly killing himself. He stayed at the Abbey for just over a year, becoming Crowley's magical student and occasional sex magick partner. Sex with Crowley was not to the young man's taste and he experienced bouts of dissatisfaction and irrationality which isolated him from those around him.

After one altercation with Crowley, who insisted that he surrender his room to new arrival Frank Bennett, Russell took himself off to live on the edge of a nearby cliff and refused food and water for several days. Soon after this he left the community for good, only to turn up later in the history of occult subculture as a proponent of unique theories of health and sensual yoga.

New arrival Frank Bennett was another longtime admirer of Crowley's writings. Originally from Lancashire, England he had emigrated to Australia and become quite a successful businessman in the building trade. Bennett stayed in touch with Crowley and Charles Stansfield Jones through written correspondence and in 1915 had gained permission to run the first OTO lodge in Australia. His organizational skills were of great benefit to the OTO cause and throughout the years of the First World War Bennett promoted Crowley's works through a series of public lectures which swelled the membership.

In many ways Frank Bennett seems to have gained the most satisfaction from his involvement with the community. During his six months of residency he attained a level of insight into the mysteries of magick and sex which satisfied his expectations. Crowley wrote Liber Samekh for Bennett, an adaptation of a fragmentary Chaldean conjuration full of barbarous names in the research papers of the Order of the Golden Dawn. This, as Crowley fashioned it, is designed to put the individual in touch with his Holy Guardian Angel.

In December of 1921 Bennett left to return to Australia having acquired a heroin dependency from his association with Crowley only to find himself estranged from his wife and son who rejected him. He continued to promote the OTO in Australia but was closed down due to pressures exerted on him by the authorities who threatened to ruin him professionally. He dissolved the small OTO and A.'. A.'. group he had gathered around him and lost touch with his brothers and sisters in Thelema, dying in 1930.

Earlier in the year, Crowley had taken a break

away from the Abbey to visit Paris in an early attempt to explore a cure for his heroin addiction. He had been prescribed this drug by his doctor some years before as a treatment for the chronic asthma which had plagued him for years. Inevitably the cure soon became a real problem and Crowley was hooked for life.

After a brief affair with the wife of a disinterested businessman, Crowley fortuitously met with Mary Butts, a rising literary star feted by Ezra Pound and T.S. Eliot who was staying in Paris with her paramour Cecil Maitland. The Beast did what he could to persuade Mary and Cecil to visit his commune and enjoy the freedoms of the New Aeon. Three months later they joined him.

By this time the magician had taken the oath of Ipsissimus, the highest grade attainable in Crowley's magical system. As usually occurs following any genuine initiation, Crowley became temporarily unstable. Despite his powerful intellect, this period of his life saw him descend into an even deeper unpredictability than usual.

During their three month stay at the Abbey, Mary Butts and Cecil Maitland reportedly witnessed Leah attempting to copulate with a goat which was then ritually sacrificed; were fed cakes of light composed of menstrual blood and practiced the most elementary rites of Golden Dawn magic such as the ritual of the pentagram.

On one occasion Crowley involved Maitland, the son on an Anglican clergyman, in a ritual involving the sacrifice of a cockerel. Life was rarely boring at the Abbey of Thelema.

Leah reveled in her role as Scarlet Woman to the Beast 666 and wrote in her 1921 diary: "I dedicate myself wholly to The Great Work. I will work for wickedness, I will kill my heart, I will be shameless before all men, I will freely prostitute my body to all creatures".

In the years following the foundation of the Abbey, Crowley and Leah made regular trips to Paris and London. His reputation had not yet reached an all-time low, despite making a name for himself as a 'traitor', and no attempts were made to arrest him at Customs when entering England. Events about to unfold at the Abbey of Thelema were to ensure that Crowley's popularity was about to take an even lower nose-dive. Within two years he would be celebrated as 'the most evil man alive', a 'human cannibal' and 'the wickedest man in the world'.

During 1922, on a visit to London where he hoped to raise an advance on the manuscript of his autobiography, Crowley did succeed in persuadingcole *Collins* to forward a fee of sixty pounds on a pulp fiction potboiler eventually published under the title *Diary of a Drug Fiend*. Crowley dashed back to his rented rooms and spent the majority of the next month dictating the tale to Leah who sat at the typewriter. Within the month he presented the finished typescript to *Collins* who were amazed that such a feat could be performed so swiftly after the original commission. The book was rushed through the publication process and became a minor success.

Unfortunately, Crowley closely modeled the story's main characters that fall into the clutches of cocaine addiction upon Cecil Maitland and Mary Butts who were incensed to find themselves so honestly depicted. This would have serious consequences when things turned ugly for the Beast following the death of Raul Loveday early the following year.

Loveday was a young Oxford graduate who had

recently married Betty May Golding, a beautiful and controversial artists model who had earned the nickname Tiger Woman from the Paris street gangs she had rubbed shoulders with during her younger days.

After meeting the Beast in London in late 1922, Loveday disappeared from his wife's side for two nights in a row after visiting Crowley and turned up again by climbing through Betty May's window smelling of brandy and ether. From this point on he was Crowley's man. Soon after this Betty May opened the door to find the magician presenting a bottle of fine wine. "I've come to dinner," he announced. She replied "I'm not cooking dinner for you," and grabbed her hat and coat moving to rush past him out of the apartment.

"One day you will be delighted to cook all my meals," Crowley answered. The arrogance of the man was insufferable.

Betty May eventually warmed to Crowley but continued to be wary about his influence over her husband who turned down a job offering a thousand pounds a year and decided to follow his master to Cefalu.

When the couple did make their journey Raoul

was in very poor health. They stayed with Nina Hamnett, a Welsh artist and writer who had made a name for herself in Paris as the Queen of Bohemia. Hamnett warned that Raoul was far too ill to go to Cefalu and that, if he did go, he would never return. She proved to be right.

On February 16th 1923 Raoul died of enteritis. The circumstances of his demise were the cause of the great outrage and campaigns of vilification aimed against Crowley in the popular press and from which his reputation would never recover.

After a period of magical study with his new master Raoul established himself as Crowley's favourite disciple. However, life at the Abbey of Thelema was rapidly becoming psychologically traumatizing.

Whilst Raoul and Betty May were resident in Cefalu Alma, Leah's sister, arrived from the States and was horrified by the poor sanitation and drug fuelled habits of the Thelemites. She took Leah's son back to America and looked after him for the remainder of his childhood. In the meantime Ninette was pregnant with Crowley's daughter Astarte Lulu Panthea which caused some friction with Leah, the Beast's official Scarlet Woman. Leah's baby daughter Poupee had died the previous winter, less than eight months old, and she was destined to miscarry another unborn child of her magical consort in the days following this event.

Helene Fraux, Ninette's sister, was as perturbed by the living conditions as Alma Hirsig and made a point of reporting the various immoralities she had witnessed to the authorities in Palermo. They sent police to investigate, but the Abbey residents had cleaned up their act sufficiently to pass the inspection.

It was around this time that Crowley had been encouraging Jane Wolfe to live in a local brothel for a month, supposedly to widen her experience of sexuality. She investigated the prospect but the manager of the establishment was only interested in lodgers who would work in the establishment. Jane declined this opportunity but attempted to make herself available for private engagements. For a while, she interested the landlord of the Villa to the extent that he introduced her to a number of prospective clients. None took up her offers and the only result of the exercise was to provide Crowley's critics in the press with the opportunity to hang charges of pimping over him.

Raoul Loveday died following the performance of a magical ritual in which he was invited to drink the blood of a black cat which was sacrificed by Crowley. Whether or not the drinking of this animal's blood contributed to the swift demise of the young acolyte is still a matter which is open to question. Raoul was in the habit of drinking the untreated local water and this could easily have been the cause of his fatal illness. However, the whole concept of sacrificing a cat and engaging in such primitive behavior did the cause of Thelema no good whatsoever.

The Newspapers on both sides of the Atlantic carried the story of Raoul's death. Betty May returned to England and spilled the beans concerning the sacrifice of the black cat. Mary Butts paid Crowley back for his mean literary depiction of Cecil Maitland and herself by tipping off the Daily Express concerning the incident where Leah had been encouraged to copulate with a goat and recounted her experiences amongst drug-taking sodomites. The public were primed to bay for Crowley's blood and the lifelong reputation for infamy which he had been so careful to cultivate began to grind into work against him.

Not surprisingly, the Sicilian authorities soon asked Crowley to vacate the island. He did so, taing Leah to Tunisia, only months later abandoning to take up with a rich American heiress Dorothy Olson leaving his students and followers to fend for themselves.

One of these dedicated followers was Norman Mudd who had abandoned a career as Professor of Mathematics to study with Crowley. Mudd was a real intellectual who had turned aside from Crowley under pressure from the university faculty. This had been during the period when fellow Cambridge scholar Victor Neuberg had invited the Beast to lecture to the student body in 1910. Later in life Mudd had regrets and donated his life savings to Crowley in exchange for the opportunity to serve him as secretary. Sadly, a secretary was all Crowley required at the time and Mudd's intellectual debates concerning Crowley's philosophy of Thelema fell on deaf ears and simply served to annoy the Master.

During the Beast's final year in Cefalu Theodore Reuss had written to Crowley in his capacity as Grand Master of the OTO pointedly asking him to drop the Thelemic elements which the English Grandmaster had written into the order's rituals and to delete all mention of the gods of *The Book of the Law* such as Ra Hoor and Nuit. Reuss wanted the OTO 'system' to be taught according to its traditional standards. Crowley's response was to declare himself the new world leader of the Order simply by making a diary entry to that effect and replying to Reuss that his days as Grand Master were at an end. Reuss died soon afterwards.

For most of the remainder of Crowley's life few real magical challenges shaped his life. His daily affairs grew ever more complex and although his literary output continued unabated there was little left for the self-proclaimed Ipsissimus to achieve.

During this period the magician believed he was transforming into a living embodiment of everything which the New Aeon of Horus stood for. Some believe that Crowley was literally possessed by a demon. Few consider the notion, as he believed, that he was possessed by the Zeitgeist, the spirit of the coming age.

A career as World Teacher did not come with a salary and the Master was forever afterwards dependent upon the financial support of his followers.

Fortunately for Crowley, his admirers were more often than not people of high finance, title or political influence. By the early 1920s he was able to draw small amounts from the trust fund he had set up for his daughter Lola Zaza and himself after his divorce from Rose. Near the end of the decade he asked his student and financial executor Gerald Yorke if he might have access to the whole fund now that Lola had come into her mother's inheritance. Yorke, a true English gentleman refused this point blank.

During the 1920s, Crowley paid two visits to Gurdjieff's Prieure in Fontainebleau; once on February 10th 1924 and finally during July 1926. The first visit occurred whilst the Russian mage was visiting America lecturing on the east coast and the Beast was greeted by one of Gurdjieff's leading pupils Major Frank Pinder. Another notable visitor to the establishment was D.H. Lawrence who thought the Prieure was a *"rotten, false, self-conscious place of people playing a sickly stunt"*. Crowley was impressed and wrote in his journal: *"Gurdjieff, their prophet, seems a tip-top man. Heard more sense and insight than I've done for years."*

He returned just over two years later with Gerald Yorke, his most enduring friend and financier, for a meeting with the master himself. Yorke, the sole witness to this meeting reports that the two got along amicably but sniffed around one another like two dogs.

Crowley was seeking the space to once again try to wean himself off his Heroin addiction. It is unlikely that Crowley would have fitted into the almost clockwork work regime that Gurdjieff insisted upon. At one time he commanded his students to cut up a huge lawn in inch square pieces and reconstruct it perfectly, piece by piece, in another spot. It is also questionable whether he would have been able to avoid friction with the majority of students at the Prieure who were fanatic about interpreting Gurdjieff's wishes literally.

When J.G. Bennett and his wife arrived to commence their studies they were shocked to find the kitchen in a state of dilapidation and general filth. The other students told them that this was the way they had found the place and assumed that this is how Gurdjieff wanted it kept. Mrs Bennett rolled up her sleeves and cleaned the scullery from top to bottom after which the Russian master teased the incumbents for their lack of initiative. He also employed a Russian peasant who only seemed to walk around criticizing everyone's efforts. When the students complained, Gurdjieff informed them that this was the man's job.

There was probably only room for one enigmatic Master in this particular commune and the position was already taken.

Israel Regardie, a young American enthusiast of Magic, Rosicrucianism and the new theories of Psychotherapy joined Crowley in Paris during 1929 as a volunteer secretary. Having being greeted at the train station by his new mentor and invited to dine with the Beast and his Scarlet Woman, Regardie was surprised to witness Crowley launch into sexual intercourse with his mistress on the carpet beside the dinner table instead of partaking of the usual cheese and biscuits. The Beast continued to remain controversial and sexually vibrant until the last day of his life.

Regardie helped his new employer knock the rough edges from the final proofs of *Magick in Theory and Practice*, Crowley's literary masterpiece of esoteric instruction. This appeared in 1929 and was well received by critics and the occult press.

In the years since the heyday of the Abbey of Thelema many of the original Thelemites had fled from their master. CF Russell had completely disavowed Crowley, Leah had been driven into penury and prostitution and poor

Norman Mudd had remained true to the last, spending the last of his energies and savings on travelling to England and printing pamphlets defending Crowley from the charges of infamy laid at his door by the Sunday Express and John Bull. Since Crowley's expulsion from Italy, Mudd had fallen in love with Leah and even participated with her in a Thelemic wedding ceremony after which they banqueted on figs. His diaries trace his final days living in the largest doss-house for the homeless in the East End of London.

Exhausted by the thanklessness of the task of representing his master, Mudd had filled his pockets with pebbles from the beach and walked into the sea to commit suicide.

By this time Crowley's literary career was in tatters. He continued to submit articles for the English Review, one of the very few journals willing to consider his written pieces, but was forced to form his own publishing company funded mainly by Gerald Yorke' in order to ensure that his books saw the light of day.

This company, The Mandrake Press, folded after only eighteen months managing to issue a favourable life study of the magician entitled The Legend of Aleister Crowley amongst a variety of books by fresh talent including The Paintings of D.H. Lawrence.

In 1930, frustrated by his lack of success in the world of publishing Crowley turned to his Art. Impressed with the German Grotesque and Da Da movements, he began to paint canvasses for display in Berlin and spent much time promoting himself there during the final years of freedom enjoyed in the Weimar Republic.

As usual a regularly changing cast of Scarlet Women assisted him in rites of sex magick, although the desired results of these operations lacked the cosmic scale of Crowley's previous ambitions. These operations of orgasm-inspired magick were nearly always focused upon gaining financial reward or inspiration for literary success.

The rise of the Nazis in Germany put paid to the Beast's artistic ambitions. Before then he rubbed shoulders with Berlin's highly political artistic elite and also made friends amongst British residents of the city such as Christopher Isherwood whose work and lifestyle inspired the film *Cabaret*.

Since the mid-1920s the bulk of Crowley's income was paid to him in the form of an allowance by Karl Germer, a rich German industrialist. To the exasperation of Germer's wife Crowley spent more per month on cigars, taxis and dining out than she received in household expenses and clothing allowance. When the Nazi administration closed down all Freemasonic and Secret Societies, Germer was imprisoned for a few months in a Gestapo basement cell where he was kept in solitary confinement. He later reported that only the knowledge and conversation of his Holy Guardian Angel kept him sane.

Crowley's lifestyle during his Berlin period has been the subject of a recent study by Tobias Churton which provides a definitive account and also raises serious questions concerning Crowley's role in subversive counter intelligence. There were reportedly instances when Crowley attempted to promote his philosophy of Thelema as a kind of super-communism and some think he used this as a cover story to ingratiate himself with left wing revolutionary elements in Berlin.

Returning to England to escape the wrath of the incoming Nazi administration Crowley launched an unsuccessful libel action against his old friend Nina Hamnett whom he considered had described him in unfavorable terms in her autobiography *Laughing Torso*. The Beast had obtained a favourable out of court decision earlier in the decade against a bookseller who dared to display a handwritten note attached to a window copy of Moonchild, intimating that Crowley's last novel had been withdrawn due to scandalous content. This minor legal success led to Crowley pocketing fifty pounds in agreed damages. In his litigation against Nina Hamnett's publishers Constable & Co he was not so lucky and the failure to prove his case led to official bankruptcy.

Justice Swift, who tried the case was shocked by the witness accounts of those who knew Crowley and also by the content of the poet's early pornographic works which were entered in evidence by the defense. He commented:

"I have been over forty years engaged in the

administration of the law in one capacity or another. I thought that I knew of every conceivable form of wickedness. I thought that everything which was vicious and bad had been produced at one time or another before me. I have learnt in this case that we can always learn something more if we live long enough. I have never heard such dreadful, horrible, blasphemous and abominable stuff as that which has been produced by the man who describes himself to you as the greatest living poet."

As far as England was concerned, Crowley was finished. Luckily he still had admirers in the United States including his old friend and disciple Jane Wolfe who was now deeply involved with W.T. Smith. Smith was an aficionado of Crowley's teachings who had more or less singlehandedly kept the OTO flag flying on the west coast of America and who continued to forward funds to the ageing magus during this time of need. The Beast was not completely enthralled with Smith's methods of management, although much of this was possible due to jealousy that Smith had proved to be so effective in attracting new members to the Order. Smith had registered The Church of Thelema as an official tax exempt religious organization in the state of California in the same year as Crowley began his legal action against Hamnett.

By the close of the 1930s England was at war against Germany and Crowley managed to raise some patriotic enthusiasm against the Nazi foe. For two years now he had been working on the designs of a new set of Tarot cards, the Thoth deck, with the Artist Frieda Lady Harris the wife of a Liberal Party member of parliament.

Harris was a talented painter conversant with the recent style of exposition known as Projective Synthetic Geometry originally developed by the artists Olive Whicher & George Adams. Expressions of this new approach to movement and depth in Art are evidenced throughout the Thoth deck and enrich the motifs to lend an almost digital edge to the imagery.

The project itself took nearly five years before completion and final publication in book form. Many of the images remained in black and white reproduction, as displayed in the rear pages of the book, until a full colour version of the deck was published in the United States during the late 1960s by Samuel Weiser &

Company.

Neither lived to see this event, but Harris successfully exhibited in Berkley Galleries in London and Crowley obtained the funds from his American followers to publish *The Book of Thoth* as a stray edition of his journal The Equinox in 1944.

By this time Crowley was a resident of Netherwood retirement home in Hastings, Sussex where he would later die peacefully in 1947 at the age of seventy two.

One regular visitor was Major Grady Louis McMurtry, an American Army Reserve officer who was stationed in England during late 1943 and early 1944. McMurtry was a First Degree initiate of W.T. Smith's Agape lodge of the OTO and had been called to duty in Normandy as a part of the invading armed forces.

He played Chess with Crowley and studied Magick directly under the Master, who later wrote to him suggesting the young man as a possible successor, or Caliph. Crowley also sent a letter conferring McMurtry to act with emergency powers if the OTO were to fall into times of trouble.

In the end, Crowley appointed Karl Germer to

succeed him as OTO Grandmaster. McMurtry eventually fell out with Germer who had ceased to initiate new members in the years following Crowley's death and actively campaigned against this policy throughout the late 1950s. Germer's representative Dr. Gabriel Montenegro ordered McMurtry to cease and desist. A decade later, following Germer's demise, McMurtry launched his own power play for the leadership with some success in the California courts.

Clifford Bax, who had brought Crowley together with Frieda Harris, now introduced him to John Symonds who became one of the literary executors named in the occult master's last testament. He was later to write a serious biography of Crowley which fails to be fully appreciated by those who only wish to read wholesome reports about their hero. Symonds account may be critical, but it admirably succeeds in conveying a sense of Crowley's mythic sense of purpose.

The final few years of the elderly magician's life was blighted with news of the problematic affairs of the Californian OTO. W.T. Smith had been Crowley's right hand man in the United

States for some time, having originally joined both the OTO and the A.'. A.'. under Charles Stansfield Jones in Vancouver over twenty years before. After following Jones to Detroit he had worked with him to establish the law of Thelema in the city before moving on to form a close association with Jane Wolfe in California.

Maverick rocket fuel scientist Jack Parsons had joined the California lodge in 1939 and made available a large mansion which he had inherited from his father for OTO meetings, performances of the Gnostic Mass and wife swapping parties. Smith was a master of all three arenas and soon claimed Parsons' wife Helen for himself. In response, Parsons took Helen's younger sister Sara, known familiarly as Betty. Betty turned out to be a highly mentally unstable troublemaker. During OTO lodge meetings she would go out to a restaurant with her friends and disrupt the ritual by having members of her party call the house telephone and ask to speak to various members in attendance. L. Ron Hubbard, founder of *Scientology* and author of the bestselling work *Dianetics* spent some months renting rooms at the Pasadena mansion and worked closely with Jack Parsons on a series of visionary experiments. He also fell in love with Betty and was unfortunate enough to become entangled in her machinations to ruin her husband financially.

A simple business deal involving Betty and Hubbard travelling to South America to buy cheap yachts for resale at much higher prices on the west coast turned into a magical duel. Parsons had parted with over twenty thousand dollars and began to fear that he had lost his life savings. Hubbard did what he could to reassure Jack when he telephoned to report the progress of the operation and Parsons was temporarily mollified. When days of silence thereafter turned into weeks, his nerve broke and he performed a ritual which raised a storm which blew the missing couple back into port.

Jack flew south to meet them and arranged the sale of two of the yachts in order to reclaim most of his funds, letting Hubbard and Betty keep one for themselves.

It is unlikely that Hubbard had entered into these dealings with anything less than good intentions. The monies he was able to raise towards the enterprise amounted to only a little over a thousand dollars, but it was everything he had. As an ex naval officer it is unlikely that he imagined that he would get away with sailing a registered yacht around the Caribbean without detection and he was certainly no fool.

Few commentators appreciate the poisonous influence of Sara 'Betty' Northrup Hollister upon the lives of both Parsons and Hubbard. The former was lucky to be so easily rid of her. Hubbard was to regret ever having met her and, despite her early secretarial help in compiling Hubbard's book Dianetics from his notes recorded on Dictaphone, she caused ongoing troubles for him in a variety of professional areas for years afterwards. Karl Germer, Crowley's chosen successor as Grandmaster of the OTO described Betty as a real-life vampire.

In the early 1940s Crowley wrote to W.T. Smith to inform him that he had examined his horoscope and discovered that Smith was becoming a living god. Furthermore, he ordered him to resign himself from the offices of the Californian lodge and take himself alone into the desert to meditate upon his initiation. Parsons was to be appointed the new leader of the Pasedena chapter.

Ever since his early visionary experiments with

Hubbard, Parsons had been performing rituals to manifest the ideal of the Scarlet Woman in physical form. Immediately after his first attempt at bringing about this desired result Jane Marjory Cameron had visited the OTO mansion. Parsons fell in love immediately and continued to practice sex magick, unknown to his new lover, with the intention of strengthening the Babalon current.

Crowley received the news of these events first hand in correspondence from Jack. In his replies to the young rocket scientist he was sympathetic; though discussing these affairs in correspondence with Germer he expressed despair, writing: "I get fairly frantic when I contemplate the idiocy of these louts."

In early 1947 Crowley was introduced to Gerald Gardner, currently considered the founding father of modern Wicca. Gardner recruited Crowley's aid in helping to lay the foundations of a modern day nature religion and paid him fifty guineas for a charter membership of the OTO. Many phrases and themes from Crowley's Book of the Law were borrowed wholesale by Gardner for inclusion in his witches Book of Shadows although many of the rites have now been rewritten by the hand of modern practitioners who find all association with Crowley and his magic slightly distasteful and inconvenient.

Before he died Crowley suggested to Karl Germer that the OTO should be wound down after his death. In one of his final pieces of writing he suggest that the doors of the temples should be closed and those of the laboratories opened. Perhaps he had visions of the kind of Machiavellian politics which lay ahead for the OTO.

Aleister Crowley breathed his last on December 1st 1947 and was cremated at Brighton Cemetary on December 5th. He had joked, quite accurately, that journalists were waiting in the bushes for him to die. According to reliable sources his final words, were "Sometimes I hate myself."

At his funeral Louis Marlowe Wilkinson, his literary executor, read the Hymn to Pan he had penned in Moscow early in the second decade of the twentieth century. Brighton Council vowed it would never allow such a shocking breach of funeral etiquette to be staged ever again.

Aleister Crowley: Man, Myth & Magick

Hymn to Pan

Thrill with lissome lust of the light,
O man ! My man !
Come careering out of the night
Of Pan ! Io Pan .
Io Pan ! Io Pan ! Come over the sea
From Sicily and from Arcady !
Roaming as Bacchus, with fauns and pards
And nymphs and styrs for thy guards,
On a milk-white ass, come over the sea
To me, to me,
Coem with Apollo in bridal dress
(Spheperdess and pythoness)
Come with Artemis, silken shod,
And wash thy white thigh, beautiful God,
In the moon, of the woods, on the marble mount,
The dimpled dawn of of the amber fount !
Dip the purple of passionate prayer
In the crimson shrine, the scarlet snare,
The soul that startles in eyes of blue
To watch thy wantoness weeping through
The tangled grove, the gnarled bole
Of the living tree that is spirit and soul
And body and brain -come over the sea,
(Io Pan ! Io Pan !)

Steven Ashe

Devil or god, to me, to me,
My man ! my man !
Come with trumpets sounding shrill
Over the hill !
Come with drums low muttering
From the spring !
Come with flute and come with pipe !
Am I not ripe ?
I, who wait and writhe and wrestle
With air that hath no boughs to nestle
My body, weary of empty clasp,
Strong as a lion, and sharp as an asp-
Come, O come !
I am numb
With the lonely lust of devildom.
Thrust the sword through the galling fetter,
All devourer, all begetter;
Give me the sign of the Open Eye
And the token erect of thorny thigh
And the word of madness and mystery,
O pan ! Io Pan !
Io Pan ! Io Pan ! Pan Pan ! Pan,
I am a man:
Do as thou wilt, as a great god can,
O Pan ! Io Pan !
Io pan ! Io Pan Pan ! Iam awake
In the grip of the snake.

Aleister Crowley: Man, Myth & Magick

The eagle slashes with beak and claw;
The gods withdraw:
The great beasts come, Io Pan ! I am borne
To death on the horn
Of the Unicorn.
I am Pan ! Io Pan ! Io Pan Pan ! Pan !
I am thy mate, I am thy man,
Goat of thy flock, I am gold , I am god,
Flesh to thy bone, flower to thy rod.
With hoofs of steel I race on the rocks
Through solstice stubborn to equinox.
And I rave; and I rape and I rip and I rend
Everlasting, world without end.
Mannikin, maiden, maenad, man,
In the might of Pan.
Io Pan ! Io Pan Pan ! Pan ! Io Pan !

Steven Ashe

Lightning Source UK Ltd.
Milton Keynes UK
UKOW04f0050281115

263671UK00001B/84/P